Joined by Fate:

INTERTWINED BIOGRAPHIES

SACAGAWEA, MERIWETHER LEWIS, AND WILLIAM CLARK

Joined by Fate:

INTERTWINED BIOGRAPHIES

SACAGAWEA, MERIWETHER LEWIS, AND WILLIAM CLARK

SHEILA LLANAS

Enslow Publishing
101 W. 23rd Street
Suite 240
New York, NY 10011
USA
enslow.com

Published in 2019 by Enslow Publishing, LLC.
101 W. 23rd Street, Suite 240, New York, NY 10011

Library of Congress Cataloging-in-Publication Data

Names: Llanas, Sheila, author.
Title: Sacagawea, Meriwether Lewis, and William Clark / Sheila Llanas.
Description: Enslow : New York, 2019. | Series: Joined by fate: intertwined biographies | Includes bibliographical references and index. | Audience: Grades 7 to 12.
Identifiers: LCCN 2017054109| ISBN 9780766098183 (library bound) | ISBN 9780766098190 (pbk.)
Subjects: LCSH: Lewis and Clark Expedition (1804–1806) | Sacagawea. | Lewis, Meriwether, 1774–1809. | Clark, William, 1770–1838. | West (U.S.)—Discovery and exploration. | Shoshoni women—Biography. | Shoshoni Indians—Biography. | Explorers—West (U.S.)—Biography.
Classification: LCC F592.7 .L77 2018 | DDC 917.804/2—dc23
LC record available at https://lccn.loc.gov/2017054109

Printed in the United States of America

To Our Readers: We have done our best to make sure all website addresses in this book were active and appropriate when we went to press. However, the author and the publisher have no control over and assume no liability for the material available on those websites or on any websites they may link to. Any comments or suggestions can be sent by email to customerservice@enslow.com.

Photo Credits: Cover, pp. 3 (top left), 78–79, 99 Bettmann/Getty Images; cover, p. 3 (top right) neftali/Shutterstock.com; cover, p. 3 (bottom left, right) Everett Historical/Shutterstock.com; p. 6 MPI/Archive Photos/Getty Images; pp. 12–13 Pierre Longnus/Photographer's Choice/Getty Images; pp. 16–17 Fotosearch/Archive Photos/Getty Images; pp. 18–19 Transcendental Graphics/Archive Photos/Getty Images; p. 23 Florilegius/Alamy Stock Photo; p. 26 National Archives, Records of the Office of the Quartermaster General; pp. 31, 88 Universal Images Group/Getty Images; pp. 32, 82 Library of Congress Prints and Photographs Division; p. 37 Historical Picture Archive/Corbis Historical/Getty Images; p. 38 MPI/Archive Photos/Getty Images; p. 40 Don Smetzer/Alamy Stock Photo; p. 45 Rui Elena/Shutterstock.com; p. 48 John Lambing/Alamy Stock Photo; p. 51 Hulton Archive/Getty Images; pp. 56–57 National Geographic Creative/Alamy Stock Photo; p. 58 Royal Geographical Society, London, UK/Bridgeman Images; pp. 60–61 Barcroft Media/Getty Images; pp. 64–65 Paul Fearn/Alamy Stock Photo; p. 67 Private Collection/Peter Newark American Pictures/Bridgeman Images; pp. 68–69 Danita Delimont/Gallo Images/Getty Images; p. 71 Randimal/Shutterstock.com; p. 81 Stock Montage/Archive Photos/Getty Images; p. 87 Private Collection/Peter Newark Pictures/Bridgeman Images; p. 91 Marilyn Angel Wynn/Nativestock/Getty Images; pp. 92, 103 Paul Fearn/Alamy Stock Photo; p. 93 Steve Cukrov/Shutterstock.com; p. 101 Manny Ceneta/AFP/Getty Images; p. 104 Kumar Sriskandan/Alamy Stock Photo.

CONTENTS

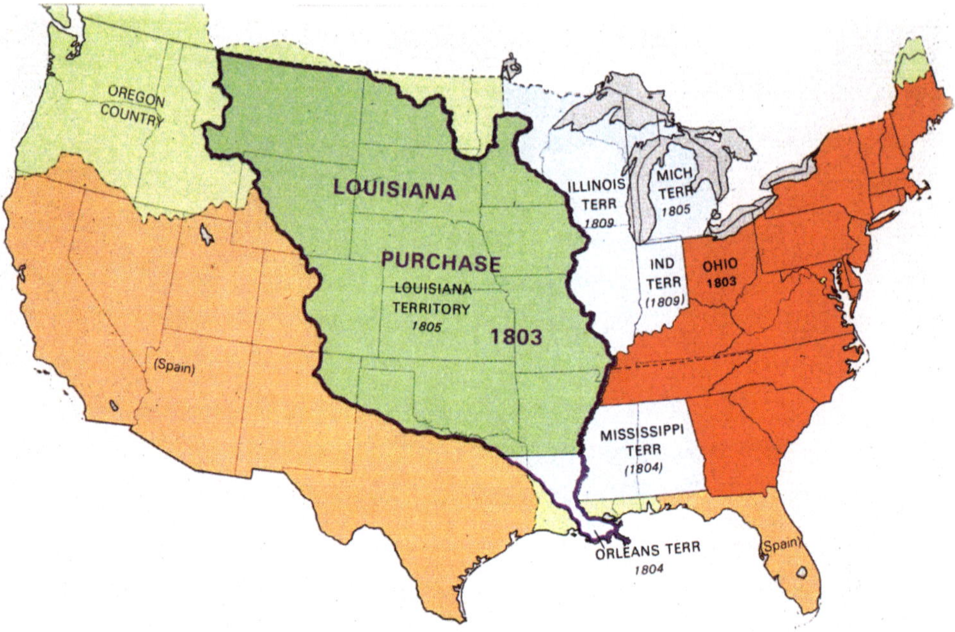

The United States doubled in size after making the Louisiana Purchase in 1803. Sacagawea, Lewis, and Clark explored this territory, home to many Native American groups.

INTRODUCTION

Captains Meriwether Lewis and William Clark crossed North America by boat, horseback, and foot during 1803–1806. They did not travel alone. They hired a fifty-man crew, as well as York, a black man Clark's family had enslaved. The crew lugged an enormous haul of supplies up the Missouri River. For this reason, historian James P. Ronda called the expedition "one of the greatest tourist attractions the native West had ever seen."[1] The expedition, called the Corps of Discovery, fulfilled President Thomas Jefferson's dream of exploring the West. Jefferson wanted to make the United States a coast-to-coast nation. And Lewis and Clark contributed to the effort by studying the plants and animals of the West, mapping the land, and getting to know the Native peoples. American Indians from Western tribes became acquainted with Lewis and Clark and their crew.

Although some had not, many Native Americans had met white people before. They'd been trading with Europeans for years. Still, this military expedition claiming to represent the United States piqued their interest, so they helped Lewis and Clark survive. They fed, clothed, and sheltered them. They offered horses and valuable geographic information. Most of the names of those indigenous people have been forgotten, but one name has become legendary—Sacagawea. This Shoshone teen, adopted into the Hidatsa tribe, had married a French trader and had a baby son.

Lewis and Clark had never imagined bringing a young woman on their journey, much less an indigenous one with a newborn child. But because she spoke two Native languages, Sacagawea joined the expedition as an interpreter. In this way, she's much like another legendary indigenous woman, La Malinche, who spoke two Native languages and helped conquistador Hernán Cortés colonize Mexico during the 1500s.

Sacagawea's journey with Lewis and Clark would not be easy. It would take two-and-a-half years to cover eight thousand miles (12,872 km) to the Pacific Ocean and back. During the journey, she endured illness, injury, and fatigue. She and the crew navigated rushing waters, freezing weather, and dangerous mountains. They confronted rattlesnakes, grizzly bears, and swarms of mosquitoes. Through it all, Lewis and Clark wrote daily journal entries describing the trip.

More than two hundred years later, their journals provide a wealth of information. As detailed as their notes are, however, they're not enough. The captains wrote very little about Sacagawea, for example. Her story has survived, in large part, because of her tribes' oral histories. As it is told and retold from both points of view, European American and Native American, it continues to be questioned and challenged. It continues to reveal insights into the making of the United States. When the lives of Sacagawea, Lewis, and Clark intersected, they became an important part of US history.

Chapter 1

BEFORE THE CORPS

Meriwether Lewis and William Clark were born in the 1770s during an exciting time. They were children during the American Revolutionary War, when George Washington became the country's first president and the Declaration of Independence was signed. Lewis and Clark both came from wealthy families. They were land-owning members of the gentry. Their ancestors immigrated to North America from England in the 1600s.[1] The Clark and Lewis families were among the first to settle in Virginia, one of the thirteen colonies in what is now the United States.

Life in the Colonies

Born on August 1, 1770, William was the ninth of John and Ann Clark's ten children. His family owned a tobacco plantation in Ladysmith, Caroline County. Meriwether was four years younger than Clark. He was born on August 18, 1774, in nearby Albemarle County. He was the middle of three children. His parents, William and Lucy Lewis, also owned a plantation. Their neighbors included Thomas Jefferson and his family.[2]

Both Meriwether and William came from military families. When the Revolutionary War started in 1775, William's five older brothers fought. So did Meriwether's father. In 1779, Meriwether's father died of pneumonia while on army leave.[3] His mother remarried and the family moved to Broad River Valley, Georgia. After the war, the Clark family also moved south—Kentucky. Both places were frontier territories. As kids, William and Meriwether learned to explore and survive in the wilderness.

They both learned a sense of responsibility. After his father died, Meriwether inherited the family estate, Locust Hill, because of primogeniture laws. These laws dictated that the eldest son received all property upon the head of

Herbalist in the Family

Lewis's mother, Lucy Meriwether Lewis Marks, was born in 1752. She practiced folk medicine. During her lifetime, few women had professional careers. But she transported homemade natural remedies by horseback to remote areas to cure illnesses. She also taught her son the medicinal qualities of wild herbs.

His mother's teachings helped Lewis care for both his men and the Native Americans he encountered on the Corps of Discovery. This knowledge proved to be immensely beneficial, as almost every Corps member, including Sacagawea, got sick at some point. Lucy Marks cared for the sick until she died, at age eighty, in 1837. Her long, healthy life stood out in a time when the average life span was just thirty-five years. She outlived her son, who died in mysterious circumstances, by eighteen years.[4]

household's death. With his new responsibilities, Meriwether left Georgia when he was about twelve years old to return to Virginia. He studied with a tutor and later managed Locust Hill. By his twenties, Meriwether was serving his country. William served in the military as well, enlisting at nineteen.

Meriwether and William had similar childhoods, which would result in them becoming great friends after they met. By a stroke of destiny, the two of them would one day meet a young Shoshone woman. As Meriwether and William began their adult lives, Sacagawea was starting her life more than two thousand miles (3,218 km) away, deep in uncharted territory.

A Shoshone Childhood

Sacagawea's upbringing could not have been more different from Meriwether's and William's childhoods. Historians mark 1788 as her birth year, but the exact date was not recorded. Her parents were Agai-Dika (Salmon-Eating) Shoshone. Her father was a chief. Her tribe lived in the Snake River Valley near the Rocky Mountains in what is now Idaho, close to the continental divide. The Shoshone tribe had lived in and around the land for thirty-five hundred years and possibly up to twelve thousand years. The nomadic Agai-Dika Shoshone moved around from one place to another along the Green, Bear, Snake, or Salmon rivers. Living in tipis made it easy for them to pack up and move often.[5]

For food, the Shoshone diet included meat. They caught fish and hunted small and large game. They could dry the fish and meat to preserve it, but they did not only eat meat. In summer and fall, groups of Shoshone women gathered seeds, such as sunflower, wild rice, and mustard. They collected roots, bulbs, and vegetables, such as ground potatoes, camas, sego lily, wild garlic, and cactus. They picked berries and, in the fall, gathered wild honey. As they worked, they talked and sang. Mothers, much like Meriwether Lewis's mother, taught their children to identify useful plants.[6]

Sacagawea had never seen a white person. No one in her tribe had. They had never traded with white French explorers, as river tribes did. To hunt food and fight enemies, the Shoshone used bows and arrows. The horses they owned allowed them to travel, but the fact that they didn't own guns forced them into hiding. Although Shoshone warriors rode horses well, their skillfulness with these animals did not protect them from armed tribes. They simply could not compete with guns.

Tribes such as the Cree, Crow, Blackfeet, and Hidatsa had been trading with Europeans for decades. Armed with European weapons, other tribes often raided Shoshone villages. They stole their food and possessions and kidnapped or killed tribal members. The Shoshone seemed to be at constant war with their neighbors. For this reason, the Shoshone tribe suffered poverty. The people often went hungry. When Sacagawea was born, the Shoshones had retreated to secluded areas in and around the Rocky Mountains.[7] In the fall, they traveled in large groups, for protection, onto the plains to hunt bison and other big game. The practice was essential to their survival, providing food, shelter, and clothing. But it was also dangerous.

Army Life: Lewis and Clark Meet

In 1791, George Washington created a volunteer army to fight the Whiskey Rebellion. Meriwether Lewis signed up. It was his first experience as a soldier. The troops marched to Western Pennsylvania, and the trek proved tough. While the officers were comfortable, enlistees lacked food, blankets, ammunition, and even shoes. In such harsh conditions, the troops gambled, drank, fought among themselves, or ran away. Such infractions were punishable by lashings.[8]

Lewis developed a taste for army life in the wild. Although he became an excellent soldier, he wasn't perfect. In 1795, he was stationed in Ohio to enforce the Treaty of Greenville. There, he was charged with unbecoming conduct for drunkenly challenging an officer to a duel during a political argument. His court martial trial returned a verdict of not guilty,[9] but the small incident had historic consequences. A guilty verdict would have led to dishonorable discharge. Instead, he joined the Chosen Rifle Company, a squad of elite sharpshooters that William Clark commanded. The two soldiers developed respect for each other.

By 1800, Clark was back in Virginia, helping his aging parents manage their plantation. Lewis stayed in the military and rose through the ranks, becoming a lieutenant and then captain. And Sacagawea was twelve years old, already promised in marriage to a Shoshone man.

Seeds of a Journey

In 1801, Lewis served as private secretary to Thomas Jefferson, the third US president. Jefferson had just negotiated the Louisiana Purchase. White Americans knew little about the Louisiana territory, the land between St. Louis, Missouri, and the Oregon territory coast. An empty patch on the map represented the area of wilderness, but the region certainly wasn't empty. Thousands of Native Americans lived there, including Sacagawea. The tribes knew the rivers, plains, mountains, and woods very well.

Jefferson wanted the land charted and explored. Since Lewis was a trustworthy and patriotic soldier, skilled in both wilderness survival and politics, the president saw him as a good choice to lead an expedition there. Lewis requested that William Clark serve as cocaptain of the expedition, known as the Corps of Discovery. Clark eagerly agreed.

The Whiskey Rebellion

To lower the national debt, in 1791 US Secretary of the Treasury Alexander Hamilton proposed taxing alcohol. When Congress passed the bill, farmers were outraged. The federal government had never taxed a domestic product before. The tax was high, nine cents per gallon (3.8 l), and had to be paid in cash. Most distillers agreed to pay. However, in Western Pennsylvania, where distilling liquor was big business, farmers did not have cash. They refused to pay and assaulted federal agents trying to collect.

President George Washington called for thirteen thousand volunteer soldiers to suppress the Whiskey Rebellion. In August 1794, he led his army of soldiers, Meriwether Lewis among them, to Pennsylvania.[10] By the time the troops reached Pittsburgh, the rebellion had ended, put down by the threat of a military invasion. In 1802, President Thomas Jefferson repealed the bill, removing the tax on liquor.[11]

During the Whiskey Rebellion, which took place from 1791–1794, Pennsylvania farmers violently attacked government tax collectors.

The army agreed to hire Clark under the lesser rank of lieutenant. Lewis made sure that no one on the expedition knew Clark's official status. He and Clark shared equal rank in every way as cocaptains.[12] The expedition stands out precisely because the two cocaptains worked so well together.

> ***"My friend I do assure you that no man lives Whith Whome I would perfur to under take Such a Trip &c. as your Self."[13]***
>
> **—Letter from Clark to Lewis, July 18, 1803**

Jefferson gave Lewis and Clark three main goals: to befriend the continent's indigenous peoples, to discover a northwest water passage, and to study the land's geography and wildlife. In reality, as Jefferson told Congress, the expedition's main purpose was commerce. The president dreamed of a coast-to-coast nation, a United States empire. He envisioned a land of pioneer farms, villages, and cities.

Native tribes occupied North America long before European explorers arrived. For thousands of years, tribal peoples lived in homelands from coast to coast.

For the United States to achieve that, Jefferson asked Lewis to establish friendly relationships with Native Americans. He believed Lewis could convince tribal people to change their way of life. He thought Native people would agree that farming a small plot of land was better than roaming the wild. He hoped that tribal chiefs would visit Washington and offered to raise and educate Native American children.[14] In service to the United States, Lewis set out to follow his president's orders, but indigenous peoples had very different ideas about what constituted a good education or lifestyle.

Chapter

2

JOURNEY'S START

Deep in the region Thomas Jefferson wanted to study, Sacagawea was almost twelve years old. As an infant, she'd been promised to wed a Shoshone man. But as Lewis and Clark prepared to explore her homeland, something happened to change her life dramatically.

Sacagawea Is Kidnapped

Sacagawea and her clan traveled to the three forks of the Missouri River, now southwest Montana. The men hunted large game, while the women and children gathered plant foods. The trip came with risks, as many tribes competed for valuable Missouri River resources. The Shoshone kept a lookout for enemies and spotted the signs of an impending raid when clouds of dust rose in the distance. Soon, warriors on horseback raced toward them. The Shoshone fled and hid. Many escaped, and a few were killed. Some were captured.[1]

Sacagawea could not escape, as one of her friends did. She was among the Shoshone caught and dragged up onto a horse. Kidnappings between tribal groups were common at the time. They not only allowed raiding tribes to increase their

The Missouri River

The Missouri River is the longest river in the United States, running for 2,341 (3,767 km) miles. The Mississippi River is a close second and almost as long at 2,320 miles (3,733 km). Formed by the confluence of three rivers, the Missouri starts in the Rocky Mountains. It ends when it flows into the Mississippi River, near St. Louis, Missouri.[2]

The Missouri is nicknamed the Big Muddy. Its waters carry the highest load of silt of any US river. The Corps used it as drinking water, but it was always muddy. It was never an easy river to travel. The river was treacherous, as its waters would abruptly change course. When sand and silt shifted, boats got caught on unexpected sandbars. In 1819, the *Independence* became the first steamboat to travel the Missouri. In the nineteenth century, two hundred steamboats sank in the river![3]

population but also their power by shaming another tribe. The warriors carried Sacagawea and other captive women and girls far from home. They made a long journey to what is today North Dakota. Sacagawea was six hundred miles (965 km) away from her Shoshone family.

Sacagawea began her new life in Metaharta, the Knife River Hidatsa village.[4] Her exact experience in those early days was not documented. However, historical information can provide context. Sacagawea's life likely resembled the lives of most Hidatsa girls and women. The Hidatsa did not always treat captives like prisoners. Sometimes, they adopted them into their tribe. Many believe that the Hidatsa gave Sacagawea her name, which means "Bird Woman." She learned the customs, geographies, and habits of the tribe.

The Mandan and Hidatsa villages were populated and bustling places, often visited by traders. Children played on the banks of the Missouri River without fear of raids or attacks.

The Hidatsa way of life differed from the Shoshone way. The Shoshone were nomadic. They moved from place to place, often when the seasons changed. They folded up their tipis like tents. Shoshone women carried the belongings, leaving men free to hunt. The tribe camped near good areas to hunt and forage for food. The Shoshones stayed near the Rocky Mountains and stuck to remote areas where few others ventured.[5] That was how Sacagawea grew up.

Unlike the Shoshone, the Hidatsa settled in permanent villages. They lived in mud lodges or huts. Outside these homes, they planted and raised fields of crops, such as corn, beans, sunflowers, and squash. In the Hidatsa culture, women oversaw crops. The Hidatsa lived along the Missouri River, a busy travel route. French traders had arrived seventy years earlier, in the 1730s. The tribe actively traded with them ever since. They saw white people all the time.[6]

Sacagawea adapted to this new culture. Because the cultures differed so, Sacagawea gained unique skill sets. She spoke both the Shoshone and Hidatsa languages. She knew two separate geographies. She didn't know it, but her new life in the Hidatsa village gave her the background needed to help with the Lewis and Clark expedition.

Preparing to Sail

As Sacagawea began her life with the Hidatsa, Captain Meriwether Lewis got ready to explore the land where she lived. Lewis learned everything he could about the tribes of the Great Plains. He studied natural history, botany, astronomy, meteorology, and topography, or map-making. Lewis was an excellent naturalist. He even mastered taxidermy, the art of stuffing an animal carcass to preserve it as lifelike. Lewis consulted expert leaders in each field.

Next, he acquired a large keelboat and loaded it with supplies, as much as the boat would hold. He brought everything he imagined he and his crew would need in the wilderness, like food, clothing, medicine, blankets, and weapons. He stocked the keelboat with flour, salt, coffee, pork, meal, corn, sugar, beans, and lard. He ordered ninety-three pounds (42 kg) of "portable soup," boiled meat, and bones dried to powder. Mixed with hot water, portable soup created broth.[7] It was a massive amount of stuff.

Lewis also brought crates filled with gifts. During the expedition, he and Clark intended to befriend the tribes they encountered. He knew that giving gifts would be a gesture of friendship. He carefully packed crates with trinkets, such as handkerchiefs, beads, ivory combs, and jewelry. He included items he knew Native people desired, such as pipe tomahawks, butcher knives, and face paint. He also packed items for tribal chiefs that represented the United States. Those items included medals printed with images of Presidents Jefferson or George Washington, flags, and paper US certificates.

Next, he needed to hire a crew. In October 1803, Lewis and Clark chose qualified men based on health, strength, and skills. The men had to know how to hunt, scout, handle boats, and survive in the wild. They'd be gone from home for more than two years, so Lewis and Clark wanted unmarried men who did not have families to support. One crewmember was an expert blacksmith and gunsmith. Others had mastered Native languages.[8] With the exception of a few French Canadians, most crewmembers were US soldiers. Along the way, the crew varied in size from thirty to fifty, and Lewis's dog, a large Newfoundland named Seaman, accompanied them.

The Corps members spent the winter near Louisville, Kentucky. They waited for spring when they could set sail. York, the enslaved man Clark brought along, served the expedition as

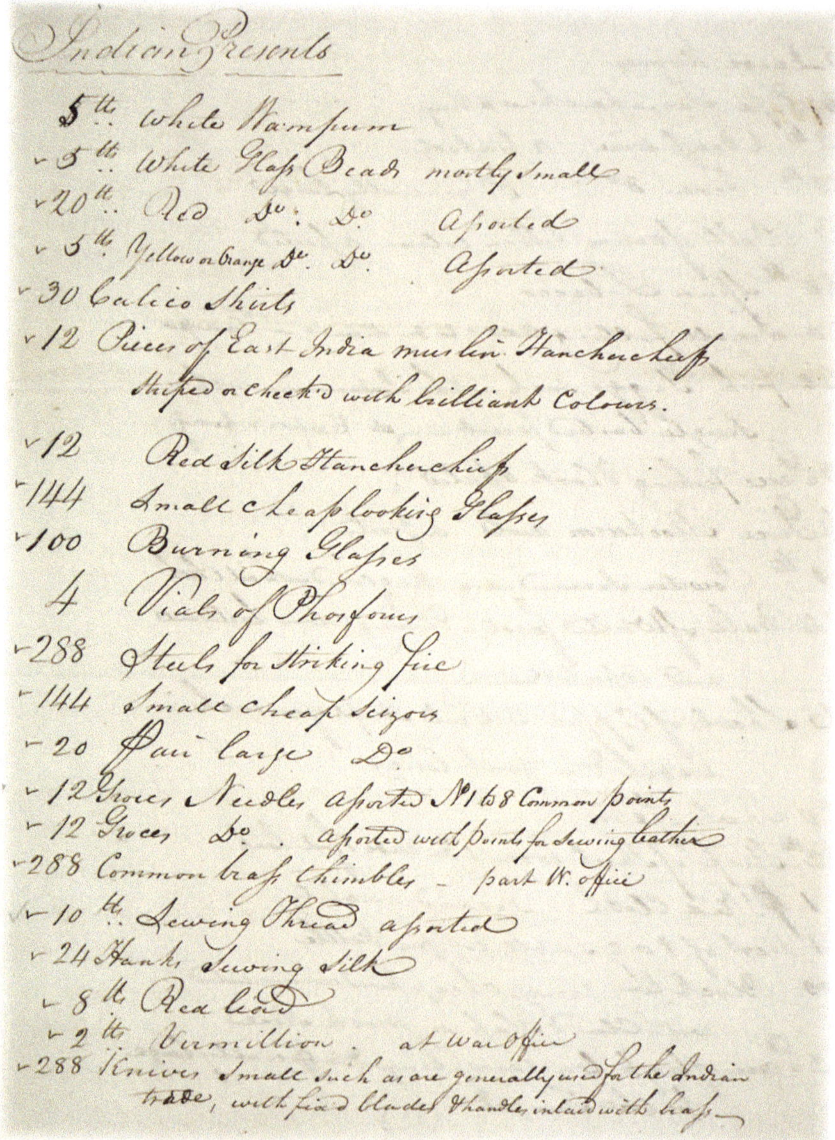

Indian Presents

5 lb. White Wampum
5 lb. White Glass Beads mostly small
20 lb. Red Do. Do. Assorted
5 lb. Yellow or Orange Do. Do. Assorted
30 Calico Shirts
12 Pieces of East India muslin Handkerchiefs striped or check'd with brilliant Colours.
12 Red Silk Handkerchiefs
144 Small cheap looking Glasses
100 Burning Glasses
4 Vials of Phosphorus
288 Steels for striking fire
144 Small cheap Scizors
20 Pair large Do.
12 Groces Needles assorted No. 1 to 8 Common points
12 Groces Do. assorted with points for sewing leather
288 Common brass thimbles – part W. office
10 lb. Sewing Thread assorted
24 Hanks Sewing Silk
8 lb. Red lead
2 lb. Vermillion . at War Office
288 Knives Small such as are generally used for the Indian trade, with fixed blades & handles inlaid with brass

Meriwether Lewis spent a third of his expedition budget on gifts for tribespeople. His purchases included pocket mirrors, ribbon, bells, brooches, and handkerchiefs.

a full crewmember. He did everything the other team members did. He cooked, set up camp, built forts, stood guard, and hauled supplies. He steered the boat, scouted unknown territory, and hunted with guns and knives.[9] At that time, enslaved people were generally barred from those activities, for they could use them as opportunities to escape.

Changes for Sacagawea, Lewis, and Clark

Sacagawea's life with the Hidatsa must have been lively. Her village was one of a cluster of five Hidatsa and Mandan villages.

York: An Amazing Crewman

York was born into slavery on the Clark plantation. Close in age, York and William Clark played together as children. As adults, Clark kept York enslaved, calling him his personal servant. York was married and perhaps had children. He did not have a say about whether he joined the expedition.[10]

Each crewmember earned double pay and 320 acres (129 ha) of land, yet York received no payment. He asked Clark for his freedom, so he could live with his wife, but Clark refused until 1815. Freed, York ran a business hauling goods with a cart and horse. He died of cholera in about 1832.[11]

Like Sacagawea, York was not able to tell his own story. No image or photo exists of him. However, a six-foot (1.8 m) bronze statue honors him in Louisville, Kentucky. On a rock ledge, holding a rifle, York appears brave, heroic, and larger than life. He faces the same river that he once traveled. York was the first African American to cross the continent from coast to coast. Today, he is remembered as a great explorer.

The population almost totaled one thousand, and other Native tribes and French traders routinely traveled the Missouri River. In 1800, she was between the ages of twelve and fourteen. At that time, she married a French trader with a checkered past named Toussaint Charbonneau. Born about 1767, he was almost twenty years older than Sacagawea. And he'd lived with the Hidatsa since 1796. The year before, a Saultier woman had reportedly stabbed him for raping her daughter.

It's not exactly clear how Charbonneau's marriage to Sacagawea came about. While it was not unheard of at this time for a girl so young to marry, most young women married when they were several years older than Sacagawea. Charbonneau might have purchased her or traded something for her, or the Hidatsa might have given Sacagawea to him. He called her and another Shoshone girl his wives. In all, he would have at least five Native American wives, all young teens.

In the summer of 1804, Sacagawea became pregnant with her first child. She lived with Charbonneau in a village along the Knife River. There, the Hidatsa kept careful watch of the larger Missouri River. They knew when travelers approached the villages. Using oral messages, travel, and sign language, they shared news up and down the river. When the Corps of Discovery floated up the Missouri, the Hidatsa and Manda people were waiting for them.

The Corps set sail on May 14, 1804. Traveling upstream was grueling. On good days, they advanced as far as twenty miles (32 km). On bad days, only one (0.6 km). After only two days on the water, the keelboat rocked unsteadily and needed to be reloaded for balance. The Corps stopped in St. Charles, Missouri, a small frontier town, populated by four hundred-and-fifty people of French Canadian descent.

From the start, Lewis and Clark, plus three sergeants, kept daily journals of events. Other expedition members—Charles

Floyd, Patrick Gass, John Ordway, and Joseph Whitehouse—kept journals as well. As ethnographers, their observations of human nature carried great importance. But sometimes Lewis's and Clark's entries differed from each other to an extent.

The captains had unique personalities and filtered their observations through their backgrounds, beliefs, and values. In a short time, Lewis and Clark would observe the behaviors of Native American groups—cultures different from their own. There, in St. Charles, on the edge of the frontier, Lewis's prejudice of people different from him surfaced. For example, he described Native peoples as "lawless savages."[12] As he became better acquainted with indigenous peoples, his beliefs would change. He would later observe that American Indians had their own laws, strong beliefs about right and wrong, and upheld values of honesty and loyalty.

To make the expedition a success, Lewis and Clark tried to maintain order in the wilderness. The captains followed military rules. When one crewmember ran away, he was tried for desertion. Another crewman, caught sleeping on guard duty, was tried by court-martial. Lewis and Clark sentenced the guilty men to be lashed with a whip. The punishment helped to establish their authority. After that, the discipline problems lessened.

They faced other obstacles. Nine days into the journey, the Corps almost met with disaster. On May 23, 1804, Lewis walked along a high cliff. He slipped! To catch himself, he plunged his knife into a crevice. He hung three hundred feet (91 m) above the river. If he had fallen, it would have meant death. Clark's journal entry understated the danger. About this accident, Clark merely noted that Lewis saved himself by using a knife.

In their journals, Lewis and Clark jotted down notes about food almost daily. They did not turn to the enormous stash of food on the keelboat for their primary meals. The main course

> ***"We eat an emensity of meat; it requires 4 deer, or an elk and a deer, or one buffaloe to supply us plentifully 24 hours."*[13]**
> **—Lewis, July 13, 1805**

was fresh meat. Each man ate up to nine pounds (4 kg) of meat a day. Nine pounds! The crew hunted daily and worked tirelessly and endlessly. They pulled canoes, trekked wilderness, hunted animals, hauled heavy loads, and chopped wood. No wonder food was a priority. Physical activity made the crewmembers ravenous. They ate bison, deer, elk, antelope, and bear. Fish was an abundant food source. They ate squirrels, birds, and beaver. Beaver tail was a favorite delicacy.

Lewis and Clark Greet Native Tribes

The expedition had not traveled far up the Missouri River when Lewis and Clark encountered tribesmen. They met the Otoes first, then the Missouris, and then the Yankton Sioux. They spent a few days with each tribe. Before meeting with the Native groups, Lewis and Clark prepared a routine. It included a ritual speech and a demonstration. They put on their dress uniforms. They paraded in uniform to display military power. They demonstrated their weapons. With a long speech, they informed the indigenous peoples they met that the land now belonged to the United States. Thomas Jefferson, they declared, was their new "Great White Father." They handed out trinkets they had brought as gifts.

In return, the tribes treated the expedition men as guests. They shared food, music, and dancing. Lewis and Clark smoked

Over his fringed frontier jacket, Lewis draped a traditional Indian tippet, or shawl. Made of ermine skins, it was given to Lewis by Cameahwait, Sacagawea's brother.

Because of his hair, William Clark received the nickname "Red Head" from the tribespeople. In 1807, artist Charles Willson Peale painted Clark's portrait, displaying it in his Philadelphia museum.

peace pipes with tribal leaders and shared many conversations. These meetings required a high degree of sensitivity and diplomacy. The captains represented the United States. They tried to ensure that their mannerisms, speech, and behaviors did not offend tribal leaders. But they also expressed the United States agenda. They gave the chiefs tokens of United States sovereignty, such as American flags, Jefferson "Peace and Friendship" medals, and certificates of loyalty. Lewis and Clark asked Native leaders to agree with the new US government laws. They urged them to promise peace with the US and other tribes.

The tribal chiefs accepted the gifts, though they had no use for coins and paper. They wanted tobacco, alcohol, blankets, and weapons—goods they saw loaded on the keelboat. They listened to the speech, but they did not necessarily agree with what they heard. Lewis and Clark, they believed, were simply another group of traders. They had trouble believing that Lewis and Clark simply wanted to see the land just to explore it.[14]

In spite of misunderstandings, the encounters went smoothly. The Yankton Sioux warned Lewis and Clark that the next tribe they would meet might not be as welcoming. The Teton Sioux were a proud and fierce military tribe. They had a reputation for being hostile.

Chapter 3

WINTER IN THE MANDAN VILLAGE

The Tetons lived on the Bad River, a Missouri River tributary near present-day Pierre, South Dakota. The Tetons were experienced traders. They had traded with French and Canadian fur companies for a long time. They were aggressive about controlling the river traffic. They demanded large payments and gifts from anyone who passed their villages. If traders refused to meet their terms, they threatened them with violence.

The Teton Sioux

In September, Lewis and Clark approached the Teton villages. They hoped to make friends with the Tetons. They performed their usual routine. They gave the speech, performed the military display, and handed out gifts. The Tetons were not impressed. If the soldiers desired trade rights, they would have to offer more than trinkets.

To make the situation worse, no Corps member spoke Sioux. They used sign language to talk, which led to miscommunication and frustration. The Tetons and the Corps did not trust each other, so tensions grew. After three days, the Corps wanted to move on. They prepared to set sail, but a few Teton men tried to stop them. The tribesmen grabbed the keelboat's cable, preventing the boat from launching. It grew into a dangerously tense moment.

Suddenly, the Tetons lined the riverbanks with their arrows pointed. The Corps members readied their guns. The two groups of men were on the verge of explosive fighting. Then Black Buffalo, a Teton chief, stepped forward. He took charge of the situation. The Corps could pass, he said, in exchange for more tobacco. Lewis and Clark angrily agreed to Black Buffalo's terms. They failed to establish friendly terms with the tribe. That close call almost ended in disaster. Months later, Clark was still angry. In his journal, he called the Tetons miscreants, pirates, and savages.

> ***"These are the vilest miscreants of the savage race ..."[1]***
> **— Clark**

Heading north on the Missouri River, the Corps passed several abandoned villages. The empty villages Lewis and Clark passed had belonged to the Arikara. The tribe once boasted thirty thousand people. But during 1780–1800, it suffered epidemics of smallpox. The terrible disease, which the Europeans brought to the Americas, had ravaged many Native American tribes. Sacagawea's Shoshone people were no exception. The Arikara's population fell to as low as two thousand people. The abandoned villages were an eerie reminder of the devastation of smallpox.

On October 10, 1804, Lewis and Clark reached the tribe. The expedition spent five days with the Arikara, and the sight of York excited the tribe. The Arikara had never met a black person before and flocked to him. As Clark wrote, they examined him "from top to toe." To entertain the tribe, York

Smallpox

European traders exposed Native peoples to European diseases. American Indians had no natural immunity to smallpox, since the disease had not existed in the Americas before the Europeans arrived. The first epidemic in the Mandan Nation struck in the 1770s and spread like wildfire, killing many people.

Fifty years later, smallpox was still a major threat. It nearly destroyed some Native tribes. In 1833, a violent outbreak killed half of the two thousand Hidatsa living along the Missouri River. The Mandan were hit even harder. They had a population of eighteen hundred. After the outbreak, fewer than two hundred people remained. In 1845, for social protection and financial security, the Hidatsa and Mandan peoples merged.[2] Next, the Arikara joined them. The Mandan Hidatsa Arikara Nation is now called the Three Affiliated Tribes.

showed off his strength and jokingly told tall tales. He told them he used to be wild, that he used to eat people, especially young children. This made the tribe's children squeal with delight. The Arikara called York "Big Medicine."[3] They were not the last group of Native people to be drawn to York.

The Corps left the Arikara and kept moving. They had to find a place to camp for the winter. Icy cold and snowy conditions would make travel impossible.

Meeting Sacagawea

Along the Missouri River, two Mandan and three Hidatsa villages formed a major trading hub. The five villages had a combined population of up to six thousand, and Lewis and Clark were not the first explorers to visit them. As early as 1738, American Indians had already traded for French and Spanish goods. By 1800, the villages were called "The Marketplace of the Central Plains." The Cheyenne, Cree, Arapaho, Comanche, and Assiniboin tribes all came to trade goods for horses, animal hides, tobacco, food, weapons, and more. In this thriving hub, Lewis and Clark planned to spend the winter.[4]

All five towns shared a similar structure. Round earth lodges were built in a circle around an open space in the middle, up to four acres (1.6 ha) large. Outside its borders, tribes grew crops of corn, squash, and beans. The largest village counted 130 earth lodges. The other four held about forty lodges each.

With villages hugging the banks of the Missouri River, the Mandan and Hidatsa peoples controlled river traffic. No water travelers passed by unseen or without stopping at the villages.

No photograph or real-life portrait of Sacagawea exists. The artist of this drawing depicted her gazing into the distance, a typical stance for male explorers at the time.

In a smaller Hidatsa town, called Metaharta, Sacagawea lived with Charbonneau.

In October, the Corps began building Fort Mandan. The triangular building had eighteen-foot (5.5-m) exterior walls. On two sides, rows of small rooms met in a point. The other side held the entrance gate.

The captains met with tribal leaders and French-Canadian traders. They asked for geographic information. The tribesmen told the explorers they couldn't travel over the Rocky Mountains by water. However, the Lemhi Shoshones owned horses. If they couldn't cross the mountains by boat, they would need horses from the Shoshone.

> ***"About five oclock this evening one of the wives of Charbono was delivered of a fine boy."***[5]
> **—Lewis**

For this reason, when Lewis and Clark met Toussaint Charbonneau, they took interest. The French-Canadian trader asked to be hired as an interpreter and guide. His wife spoke the Shoshone language and could help them negotiate a horse trade. On November 4, they met Sacagawea. She was about sixteen years old. In front of her, she carried a gift of a bison robe. When she gave it to them, she revealed that she was six or seven months pregnant.

Lewis and Clark reached a verbal agreement with Charbonneau. He and Sacagawea could join the expedition, so the couple moved into Fort Mandan.[6]

A Birth at Fort Mandan

On February 11, Sacagawea went into a long and difficult labor. As the doctors of the expedition, Clark and Lewis assisted her.

Someone told Lewis that a rattlesnake's rattle would help her deliver the baby, so he crushed a bit of dried rattle, mixed the powder with water, and gave it to her to drink. Whether or not the rattlesnake remedy helped, Sacagawea's son was born ten minutes later. She named him, her first child, Jean Baptiste. Clark nicknamed the baby boy Pomp, or Pompy.

When Jean Baptiste was one month old, Charbonneau talked with Lewis and Clark. If he came along on the expedition, he said, he would not do any of the other work everyone else had to do. He refused to stand guard, cook, man the boats, or chop wood. He would help interpret and that's all. The captains denied his terms, so Charbonneau quit.

When Corps members built the high stockade walls of Fort Mandan, the Hidatsa and Mandan people watched in fascination.

River Tribes: Mandan and Hidatsa

In North Dakota, archeologists discovered a Mandan village dated as far back as 900 CE. The Hidatsa arrived later, in about 1600 CE. Over time, the Hidatsa followed the Mandan example. They settled in villages rather than move around as nomadic peoples. By 1700, the Mandan and Hidatsa, along with other tribes, thrived along the Missouri River. Camps and villages ranged from the Cannonball to the mouth of the Yellowstone. Historians estimate that, in the 1730s, as many as fifteen thousand Mandans were leading healthy lives.[7]

The Hidatsa and Mandan spoke different languages. The Mandan called themselves "people of the first man." The word Hidatsa is said to mean "willows."[8] The two tribes lived close to each other. Even as they formed an alliance, they remained separate tribes with distinct characteristics.

Lewis and Clark did not like Charbonneau very much. They said that he had "no particular merit." But they needed Sacagawea. A few weeks later, Charbonneau changed his mind. He agreed to the terms and joined the expedition. Charbonneau was the Corps's oldest member, and Sacagawea was the only woman. Their son was the youngest.

From Fort Mandan, many crew members were sent back to St. Louis, because the keelboat was too large to sail on the narrowing Missouri River. Besides, they had a lot of samples to send back to President Jefferson. Lewis and Clark loaded the boat with plants and animals they had collected. They packed maps, Indian artifacts, and other scientific specimens. They sent

Lewis, chasing him. Lewis quickly reloaded his gun and shot and killed the bear. Only then did he understand that the stories he'd heard from the Native peoples weren't myths. Grizzlies were as fierce and dangerous as the tribesmen had said. They can weigh up to nine hundred pounds (408 kg) and stand up to ten feet (3 m). Lewis and Clark may have described the bears as "grisley" because of the golden and gray tips in their fur or because of the fear the animals aroused in anyone who crossed their path. In any case, the name "grizzly" stuck for the bear, known among scientists as the North American brown bear. After a few close calls, Lewis had seen enough. His curiosity, he wrote, had been satisfied regarding the grizzly bear.[2]

The Corps rowed the pirogues and smaller canoes upriver. In rough water, the men waded in and dragged the boats upstream. Some men went on shore to hunt or scout. Sacagawea often walked onshore alongside the boats. She carried Jean Baptiste on her back. Often, Clark and a few others joined her. The Corps members got to know their newest team member well this way.

Traveling was hard work. The Corps spent much time hunting large animals for food. In that area, Sacagawea's husband, Toussaint Charbonneau, helped. He lacked wilderness skills, but he could cook. His specialty dish was called boudin blanc, sausage made with bison intestines. The special dish was a treat for the men. But it was Sacagawea who added fresh foods to their diet.

Sacagawea was new to the Corps, but she quickly balanced the meals by gathering foods. She foraged for edible plants, such as currants, wild licorice, and onions. She dug mounds of hog peanuts that mice had buried. She collected breadroot, or prairie turnip, which Lewis called white apple.[3] The men had never eaten the foods she'd found. They welcomed and needed her skills. Lewis believed he could survive on a diet of meat

Shoshone Diet

Sacagawea's people ate seeds, roots, and berries. According to tradition, her mother taught her to forage. Using digging sticks, she knew how to find edible roots and bulbs. The Shoshone ate ground potatoes, camas root, sego lily, wild garlic, and cactus. They picked berries of all kinds, collected wild honey, and gathered pine nuts. The skills Sacagawea learned from her Shoshone upbringing made a difference on the expedition. The nutrient-rich foods she gathered supplemented a diet of mostly meat.

Sacagawea supplemented the team's diet of meat by foraging for nuts, seeds, roots, and fruits. The explorers hadn't eaten these nutritious foods, which staved off disease and nutritional deficiencies.

alone, but he was wrong. To prevent diseases like scurvy, the expedition members needed the nutrients of fresh fruits and vegetables as well. As centuries have passed, a well-balanced diet remains important. Eating fruits and vegetables provides a number of health benefits.

Sacagawea's Level Head

Lewis and Clark, often in extreme conditions, wrote notes almost every day about their expedition. The journals, in their original form, are full of misspelled words. For example, Clark spelled the word "Sioux" twenty-seven different ways.[5] Although the first dictionaries of English words appeared in Britain in the 1500s, the first dictionary for American English speakers wouldn't appear until hundreds of years later. Noah Webster did not create the dictionary of American English until 1806 and 1807. There was no reference to provide a standard way to spell words, so proper spelling was not a common practice.

> ***"The want of bread I consider as trivial provided I get fat meat."*[4]**
> **—Lewis**

Lewis and Clark wrote Sacagawea's name fourteen times during the entire three years of the expedition. In other cases, they called her "Snake Woman," "the Indian woman," "our Indian," "Charbonneau's woman," or "squar." By "squar," Lewis and Clark likely meant "squaw," which today is often regarded as an offensive term to call a Native American woman.

Lewis and Clark did not have a standard way to spell Sacagawea's five-syllable name. The spelling of her name has been a topic of interest ever since. It is still written many ways, including as Sacagawea, Sacajawea, or Sakakawea.[6] Scholars have also debated about the pronunciation, whether to use a hard or soft "G" sound. On July 28, 1805, in his journal entry, Lewis tried to spell the name phonetically, or the way it sounded. "Sah-cah-gar-we-ah," he wrote. To make it easier for him to address her, and perhaps out of endearment for

Sacagawea, Clark nicknamed her "Janey." We don't know how she felt about Clark Americanizing her name in this way.

Overall, Sacagawea proved not only to be an expert food gatherer but also quite levelheaded. In May, one of the boats began to rock side to side, and it almost capsized. Charbonneau was at the helm. But because he couldn't swim, he panicked. He made the boat rock harder and almost sank it. Important items fell out into the water. While he was screaming for help, Sacagawea calmly reached out, lifted the wet things up, and placed them back in the boat. She gathered papers and medicines and other valuable goods.

Lewis praised Sacagawea for her calm actions. She showed as much strength and courage as anyone on board. On May 20, 1805, just a few days later, the captains named a stream "The Sacagawea" in her honor. Lewis called it "bird woman's River, after our interpreter the Snake woman."[7] In this journal entry, the explorer did not refer to her as Charbonneau's wife. He gave her respect by mentioning her name, the translation of her name, her role, and her Shoshone heritage.

Two months after leaving the Hidatsa village, Sacagawea grew very ill. It was June 1805, and she developed an infection. Her symptoms included fever, weak pulse, irregular breathing, and a twitching of her fingers and arms. Clark took care of her. He bled her, applied poultices, and gave her laudanum. But Sacagawea did not get better; she got worse.

Lewis wasn't around when Sacagawea fell ill. He had walked ahead to explore the river and saw an amazing sight. The Great Falls of the Missouri River rose before him. He saw not only one waterfall, but five! The magnificent waterfalls, however, meant that the Corps would have to carry the boats a great distance over land. There was no other way around them, so Lewis returned to the main camp to tell the men and prepare

A tributary of Montana's Musselshell River was named to honor Sacagawea for her bravery. It is 30 miles long and technically a stream, not a river.

for the difficult portage. When he made it back, he was alarmed to find Sacagawea close to death.

The son of a healer and herbalist, Lewis treated Sacagawea and tended to her health, along with Clark. The captains had grown fond of her. They worried about who would take care of her baby if anything happened to her. But there was a self-serving reason they cared about Sacagawea too: They needed her as an interpreter.

In his journal entry on June 16, 1805, Lewis expressed his concerns. They depended on her, he wrote, to make friendly negotiations with the Snake Indians for horses. Sacagawea might be able to guide them to the Shoshone camps. She would certainly be able to translate when they negotiated for horses. Finally, Lewis gave her water to drink from a nearby sulfur spring.[8] The medicine seemed to work. Sulfur springs can be found around the world, and even today, people soak in such water for its perceived health benefits. Soaking in the water can supposedly kill viruses, improve blood circulation, and relieve arthritis, but formal medical studies on this water have proven inconclusive. Also, doctors today warn people not to drink sulfur water like Sacagawea did, as too much can cause stomach upset. Whether sulfur water cured Sacagawea or not, her recovery relieved Lewis and Clark and the members of the expedition.

After a while, the expedition drew closer to the site of Sacagawea's capture, near the three forks of the Missouri River. The Shoshone teen was returning to the West, back to her birthplace. On July 22, 1805, she recognized the countryside as the home of her childhood. She told Captain Lewis that her relations lived nearby. Her news greatly cheered Lewis and the rest of the Corps. They were going in the right direction. The expedition had to find horses quickly to get across the mountains before winter arrived. Time was running out.

In the Medicine Kit

Health was an important aspect of the journey. Lewis did not enlist a doctor to join the trip. He would do the doctoring himself. To prepare, he got advice from Dr. Benjamin Rush. The highly esteemed doctor, one of the signers of the Declaration of Independence, prepared a list of supplies for Lewis.

Dr. Rush believed a good laxative was the cure-all for any ailment. He turned to his own creation, bilious pills, as his go-to prescription. The potent tablets had earned the nickname Thunderclappers. The laxatives were made of sixty-percent mercury. Doctors did not yet know the silver liquid metal was poisonous. Moreover, penicillin, which kills bacteria, hadn't yet been invented.[9] In fact, doctors used mercury to treat syphilis, a sexually transmitted disease that can result in death, if untreated.

Used as a laxative, the mercury mostly passed through a person's system and drained out onto the ground. Mercury does not break down. After the pills did their job, the men left traces of mercury behind. So when historians began to trace the Lewis and Clark trail, they easily mapped the location of the forts. But campsites mentioned in the journals were lost. Archeologists pinpointed "Travelor's Rest" on Lolo Creek, south of Missoula, Montana. They knew it was the right location because they'd found mercury in a latrine.[10]

Getting Past the Missouri

When the Corps entered Shoshone territory, they could not find anyone. Shoshone were known to be shy, guarded, and protective people. At the time, the tribe was as large as five hundred members. The tribe had endured decades of enemy

This photo of a Shoshone man was taken in 1900. Just a century earlier, the tribe owned little ammunition to protect themselves and their herd of horses. They hid from the expedition.

raids, periods of hunger and, more recently, a crippling smallpox epidemic. To stay safe from armed tribes and dangerous white European traders, they hid from strangers in the mountains. They survived on the wild plants they could find and the small game they caught.

The expedition drew near enough to see the mountains. The closer they got, the bigger they looked. Back in Virginia, they had imagined the Rockies were no bigger than the Appalachians. Instead, they were enormous. If the Missouri River did not, after all, connect to the Columbia, they could not cross the Rockies in canoes. They would need horses. The whole mission now depended on getting horses. To obtain the animals, they needed to trade with the Shoshone, but they had to find the tribe first. The Shoshone people rarely, if ever, interacted with whites, but Lewis, Clark, and Sacagawea would change that.

Chapter

5

MEETING THE SHOSHONE

Sacagawea must have been excited to return to her birthplace and to see her people again. There is no way to know for certain. Meriwether Lewis knew her story. He knew that she'd been kidnapped and wondered if returning to the mountains excited her.

On July 28, he wrote, "I cannot discover that she shows any emotion of sorrow in recollecting this event, or of joy in being restored to her native country; if she has enough to eat and a few trinkets to wear I believe she would be perfectly content anywhere."[1]

While Lewis isn't critical of Sacagawea in this passage, he does make assumptions about her emotional life and values. He also ignores the fact that she was a trauma survivor, who was not only kidnapped from her family and tribe but also given away in "marriage" to a man twice her age afterward. Sacagawea may have learned to survive these deeply traumatic events by not openly expressing her emotions or shutting herself off from them. Or perhaps the reality of seeing her people again had yet to sink in fully. This does not mean she was content in life with just the basics—food and clothing—as Lewis suggests. But since Sacagawea could not read his words, Lewis didn't have to worry about how she'd respond to his observations or if she'd object to them entirely. Surely in her own way, she reacted to the prospect of seeing her birthplace once again.

Lewis Goes First

Along with three Corps members, Lewis left the expedition's core group in August. He went to search for the Shoshone but, oddly, didn't invite Sacagawea to accompany him. She was the expedition's sole Shoshone member and the only one who spoke the language. It would have been sensible to bring her along. Instead, he brought George Drouillard, the Corps member who knew sign language. Lewis and Clark made plans to reunite later.

On August 12, Lewis and his party reached Lemhi Pass. They crossed the Continental Divide, something no American had done before. They left United States territory and entered lands claimed by Great Britain, Spain, and Russia. They saw a magnificent vista of jagged Rocky Mountain peaks. Finding the icy beginnings of the Missouri River thrilled Lewis. On the other side of the mountains, however, there were no running waters. His emotions quickly shifted from exuberance to dismay. The view confirmed that the Missouri and the Columbia Rivers did not connect. This meant that, instead of a short portage, the expedition would have to cross the Rockies on foot and horseback.[2] Despite this setback, Lewis remained optimistic. They'd find the Shoshone, trade for horses, and all would be well.

On August 13, Lewis spotted a Shoshone man on horseback. He called out, but the man galloped away in fear. One mile (1.6 km) later, three Shoshone women foraged in a field. On seeing the white men, they sat down on the ground, showing how

Lemhi Pass

The US government designated Lemhi Pass a National Historic Landmark in 1960. With an elevation of 7,323 feet (2,232 m), the 2-mile (3.2-km) trail crosses the Rocky Mountains along the present-day border between Montana and Idaho. In the shape of a rounded saddle, it crosses the Continental Divide. Its ridge extends north and south along Beaverhead Range.

The Forest Service maintains the area's natural, historic landscape. With sagebrush and tall grasses, stands of Douglas fir and lodge pole pine trees, the landscape is still as remote as when the Corps of Discovery crossed it. The views are stunning, although the mountain weather can be harsh and unpredictable. It can snow any time during the year. In summers, major thunderstorms pelt the pass. In 1805, Lewis and Clark crossed the pass on foot and horseback. Today, travelers can drive along a road, which can be rough and narrow, rocky and rutted. Drivers prepare with spare tires, equipment, and a full tank of gas.[3]

frightened and helpless they felt. Lewis gave them gifts of beads and vermilion face paint. He earned their trust.

The women led Lewis and his men to their village. As they approached, however, sixty Shoshone with bows and arrows raced toward them at full gallop. The lone man Lewis had seen earlier had alerted the tribe. The tribesmen were ready to overpower Lewis and his group. The scene could have quickly turned bloody if not for the Shoshone women. Luckily, the women vouched for Lewis. They displayed the gifts they'd received. Pleased, the chief dismounted and treated Lewis and his group like new friends. He gave Lewis a warm

After Shoshone women convinced their tribe that Lewis and his men were friendly, the Shoshone welcomed the Corps to their camp. Before long, Sacagawea would be reunited with the tribe she was kidnapped from in childhood.

traditional greeting. He slung his arm around Lewis's shoulder and pressed his cheek to Lewis's. One by one, the tribesmen showed Lewis and his group the same courtesy. Soon they were all smeared with grease and paint.[4]

The historic meeting was a first for both sides. The Shoshone had never seen white people, and no American had

Lewis faces Shoshone warriors for the first time. Oddly, he did not bring along his Shoshone interpreter, Sacagawea. She likely would have eased tensions simply because she spoke Shoshone.

ever seen a Shoshone war party. Despite their warm greetings, both Captain Lewis and Chief Cameahwait distrusted each other. Tension thickened when Clark and the rest of the Corps failed to appear at the meeting place on time. To reassure Chief Cameahwait, Lewis told him that a Shoshone woman and child traveled with him. The chief was curious to meet her.

A Miraculous Reunion

That same day, August 17, 1805, Clark and the rest of the Corps went to meet up with Lewis. Clark strolled along the shore with Charbonneau and Sacagawea, as he often did. They had walked about a mile (1.6 km) when they saw the Shoshone.

It was in that moment that a miraculous reunion occurred. Sacagawea saw the Shoshone, and she began to dance with joy and happiness. She turned around to look at Clark. She pointed to the Shoshone and sucked her fingers. In sign language, she was telling Clark that these were her people. She was related to them. Not only that, but a Shoshone woman recognized Sacagawea and ran to her. They embraced with affection.

The men went into a tent with the chiefs. They called for Sacagawea to translate for them. Sacagawea came in and sat down. As she began to translate, however, she burst into tears. She jumped up, rushed to the Shoshone leader, and wrapped her blanket around him. The gesture meant that she was claiming him as her family. Chief Cameahwait was her brother. They all sat down to talk, with Sacagawea interpreting. Their talk was often interrupted because Sacagawea could not stop crying. She was overcome with emotion. Indeed, she felt overjoyed to reunite with her people after several years.

Sacagawea learned that many of her family members, including her parents, had died. She met her nephew, however, Cameahwait's son. And she introduced Jean Baptiste to his Uncle Cameahwait. That day, Lewis wrote the longest journal entry he'd ever recorded about Sacagawea. He described the amazing reunion with her people.

> ***"Sacajawea ... began to dance and show every mark of the most extravagant joy, turning round him and pointing to several Indians ... sucking her fingers at the same time to indicate that they were of her native tribe."[5]***
>
> **—Lewis**

The Shoshone Today

In the 1850s, Mormons changed the Agai-Dika name to Lemhi Shoshone. At that time, pioneers flooded the West, claiming prime pieces of land and settling on Indian hunting grounds. When large game and other food sources dwindled, the Shoshone raided white farmers. One retaliation effort turned brutal. In 1863, US soldiers from Fort Douglas, Salt Lake City, made a surprise attack on a sleeping village. The Shoshone killed eighteen soldiers. The army slaughtered an estimated two hundred-and-fifty Shoshone in response. The killings became known as the Bear River Massacre.[6]

In 1875, the eighteenth US president, Ulysses S. Grant, established the Lemhi Valley Indian Reservation, a 100-square-mile (160 sq km) territory for the Shoshone, Bannock, and Sheapeater tribes. Government officials and pioneer farmers fought to end the reservation. Chief Tendoy, nephew of Cameahwait and Sacagawea, led the tribe during peace councils. He attempted to retain ownership. In 1905, the US relocated the Shoshone to the Fort Hall Indian Reservation.[7] The contract had lasted thirty years.

Today, the Shoshone population is an estimated forty-one thousand people. Eastern Shoshone live on the Wind River Indian Reservation, in Wyoming, near the Shoshone National Forest and Yellowstone National Park. Western Shoshone, however, have never been federally recognized. The tribe has struggled with legal disputes since the 1950s. They declared their own sovereignty in 1982, issuing passports through the Western Shoshone National Council.[8]

Every year, thousands of indigenous peoples gather for the annual Shoshone-Bannock Pow Wow on the Fort Hall Indian Reservation in Idaho. Pow wows offer a chance for native peoples to come together and partake in ceremonies and traditional dances.

Trading Guns for Horses

During the next few weeks, the Shoshone and the Corps talked and shared information. Communication was not easy. The translation chain was several links long. Sacagawea translated from Shoshone to Hidatsa. Her husband, who did not speak English, translated her Hidatsa words into French. Then, a French speaker would translate his words into English. In this way, the Corps and the Shoshone got to know each other.

> ***"All the nations on the Missouries below make war on them & Steal their horses."*[9]**
>
> **—Lewis**

Lewis and Clark desperately needed horses and wanted them in a hurry. They had to cross the mountains before winter. Chief Cameahwait, however, did not hurry to help the expedition. For his tribe, fall marked hunting season—the time to get meat to survive the winter. Feeding his own people took precedence over helping the Corps cross the Rockies. But this frustrated Lewis, who believed his mission outweighed the tribe's welfare.

Tension and anger built up on both sides. In the end, Lewis and Clark rapidly traded anything they could. They gave away clothing, knives, and iron axes, plus guns and ammunition, in exchange for a small herd of horses.[10]

The deal was done. The Shoshone took off for their hunt. That's when the Corps of Discovery realized that the tribe had given them the herd's weakest and youngest horses. With sore, frail backs, they could not carry packs or human riders. But the Corps had to move forward.

Chapter 6

OVER THE ROCKIES

As August ended, Lewis and Clark felt that time was running out. Before long, frigid temperatures and snow would make the Rockies impossible to cross. So they decided to say goodbye to the Shoshone and face the mountains. The Shoshone sent a guide with the expedition. His name was Old Toby, and he and his four sons would show the group the way.

It may have comforted Sacagawea to have Old Toby and his sons with them since they spoke her native language. But leaving the Shoshone camp must have been emotionally trying. She had to leave her family and friends behind once again. Did she have a choice in the matter? Did she want to stay with her husband or feel a loyalty to the expedition? Scholars and historians have wondered why she didn't stay.

Over the Continental Divide

The Corps started to cross the mountains not a moment too soon. Even as they trekked, snow began to fall. An icy sleet set in. By early September, temperatures fell below freezing. The crew cut through thick underbrush, scaled steep hills, and climbed over fallen trees. As with every part of their journey,

> *On Sept. 16, 1805, Sergeant Patrick Gass called the Rockies, "the most terrible mountains I ever beheld."*[1]

they had an enormous amount of belongings to haul and carry. The path was so rough that three of Old Toby's sons turned back and went home.

It took five days just to cross the Continental Divide. They'd gone only halfway. They were hungry and cold. Fortunately, they entered the Bitterroot Valley and came across a large camp of American Indians. A tribe of about four hundred Salish-speaking Indians lived in the valley. They were waiting for the expedition to arrive. They had been scouting the Corps for three days. At first, they feared the Corps wanted to raid them. But the white men looked too poor. They had no blankets. They marched in the open, making no effort at stealth.

Charles M. Russell's mural *Lewis and Clark Meeting the Flatheads at Ross's Hole* covers an entire wall inside Montana's capitol building in Helena.

The Lewis and Clark expedition looked defeated. The Salish people wondered if they'd been robbed[2] but didn't hesitate to welcome the weary group of travelers. They hugged them just as the Shoshone had. Next, they covered them with warm robes. For several days, they fed and sheltered them.

Sergeant John Ordway, a member of the Corps, remembered the kindness of the Salish in his journals. He described them as honest, friendly, and eager to help with the expedition.[3] Although none of the expedition participants spoke Salish, a Shoshone boy lived with the tribe. Like Sacagawea, he had been kidnapped and adopted by his new tribe. The captains set up a translation chain. The boy translated Salish into Shoshone. Sacagawea translated his words into Hidatsa for her husband. Charbonneau spoke to them in French, and a French-speaker delivered the English words to Lewis and Clark. Back and forth along this chain, Lewis and Clark spoke with the Salish people.[4] The captains asked to trade weak horses for stronger ones and finally received the healthy animals they needed to complete their journey.

On September 12, the Corps entered the most dangerous part of their journey. They used the Lolo Trail to cross the Bitterroot Mountains, a range in the Rockies. At first, the trail was clearly marked. Soon, it grew hard to find. Even their guide, Old Toby, got lost and led them out of the way. On slippery rocks, horses tripped or fell. A few packhorses got lost. The men had to spend time finding them. They could not afford to part with their supplies, but many of their belongings got lost or broken. At one point, Clark's portable writing desk fell and plunged down a rocky cliff.

In addition, the thin mountain air made it hard to breathe. Game was scarce, as animals did not live high on the ridges of the mountaintops. This meant food supplies ran low. The men ultimately killed and ate one of the horses. Because of that decision, they named a stream Killed Colt Creek.

At night, they had difficulty finding level places to camp, so they slept on the ground. One morning, they awakened to their worst fear. Eight inches (20 cm) of snow covered them in their beds on the ground.[5] That day stood out as the most miserable of the whole journey. Corps members suffered frostbite, exhaustion, and dehydration. All of these conditions could have made them gravely ill or even killed them.

The trip was supposed to take five days. Instead, the two-hundred-mile (320-km) stretch took them eleven days. When they reached the other side of the Bitterroots, they entered Weippe Prairie. It is located near what is today the Idaho-Oregon border. At this point, the expedition badly needed help.

A Token of Peace

Help came in the form of the Nez Perce. The tribe's name is French for pierced nose. Tribe members wore nose rings made of needles, shells, or other trinkets. The Nez Perce knew the Lolo Pass very well. They crossed it every year to hunt on the plains. The Nez Perce, like the Shoshone, had rarely seen white people. Not only had they never traded with them,[7] they also feared them.

"I have been wet and as cold in every part as I ever was in my life."[6]
— Clark

But Sacagawea's presence in the expedition allayed their fears. The sight of a Native

This 1938 oil painting by American artist NC Wyeth (1882–1945) shows Sacagawea pointing the way for Lewis and Clark. She guided them through the territory containing her homeland.

American woman in the group comforted the Nez Perce. Moreover, a war party would have never included a woman and a child, so seeing Sacagawea and her baby signaled that they were not in danger. Although Lewis and Clark relied on Sacagawea for translation, they did not imagine that her mere presence would have convinced the Native people they encountered that the Corps were a friendly group.

Like the Shoshone, the Nez Perce could have easily killed these white men and taken their weapons, perceiving them

Lolo Pass

The Lolo National Forest contains whitewater rapids, hot springs, and wildlife such as deer and mountain goats. Located in the Nez Perce National Historic Park, Lolo Pass sits on the Nez Perce National Historic Trail. Lewis and Clark used it once, but the Nez Perce used the trail for thousands of years, crossing from their homes in Northeast Oregon to Great Plains hunting grounds. In 1877, the Nez Perce followed the trail to escape US troops forcing them onto a reservation.[8]

With an elevation of 5,233 feet (1,595 m), Lolo Pass is the highest point of the Lolo Trail. Two hundred miles (320 km) long, the trail crosses the state border as it goes between the Bitterroot Valley in Montana and the Weippe Prairie in Idaho. Today, US Highway 12, also called the Lewis and Clark Highway, crosses Lolo Pass. From Lewiston, Idaho, to Missoula, Montana, that section of road offers a curvy winding ride through the gorgeous scenery of the Rocky Mountains. It is now a favorite ride for motorcyclists.

Today, the Lolo National Forest, west of the continental divide in western Montana, spans two million acres of diverse wilderness.

> ***"A woman with a party of men is a token of peace."*[9]**
> **— Clark**

as threats. But a Nez Perce woman named Watkuweis asked her tribe not to harm the group because white people had once helped her. Because of her, the Corps of Discovery avoided a disaster.

For two days, the Nez Perce fed the expedition their diet of dried fish and camas roots, a flowering bulb. The famished Corps members gorged on the food. Maybe they ate too much on empty stomachs. Maybe bacteria had tainted the fish. They were also not used to eating camas roots. For any of these reasons or a combination of them, the food that saved them from starvation also made them sick. Everyone except for Sacagawea grew ill with vomiting and diarrhea. Clark handed out Dr. Rush's Thunderclappers, powerful laxatives that only made their symptoms worse. For days, the men could do nothing but lie on the ground.

Although the men were sick, they had much work to do. They needed to cut trees to make new canoes. On October 6, 1805, they put them in the water. The expedition once again traveled by water, on the Columbia River. What a relief to sail downstream. Instead of dragging the boats upstream, the Corps steered through swift currents and rushing rapids. The fast-paced rapids terrified their Shoshone guide, Old Toby. He and his son left the expedition. They did not even wait to be paid. No historical record exists of what happened to them afterward.

The Corps no longer had an official guide. The canoes rushed toward the Pacific Ocean. They covered up to thirty miles (48 km) per day.[10] They neared the western edge of the continent. There, they would spend the winter. The expedition team had to decide where to build a new fort.

The Nez Perce fed starving Corps members the root of the camas flower, a food item that saved them from hunger but also made them sick.

Watkuweis

When Clark and six men were out hunting, they surprised a group of Nez Perce warriors. The Nez Perce considered overpowering them and taking their weapons. A woman of the tribe convinced them not to harm the men. An enemy tribe had captured Watkuweis, as Sacagawea had been. The Blackfeet took her to Canada, where a white man bought her. They then had a child.

After eight years as a captive, Watkuweis longed to go home to her own people. A group of white people helped her escape. They gave her a horse and food, and she made a long, difficult journey back. Her child died along the way, and her own health suffered.

Finally, she returned home to the Nez Perce. She was dying when she spoke up for Clark and his men, asking the warriors not to hurt them because of how white people had helped her.[11] Her story has been preserved through the Nez Perce tribe's oral history.

On November 23, 1905, Lewis and Clark took a vote on a location that has since become a famous historic landmark. They invited every member of the party to vote. In their journals, they recorded each person's name and how they voted, including Sacagawea and York. It reportedly marked the first time in US history that a woman and a black man voted[12] in such a manner.

A West Coast Winter

Together, they decided to build Fort Clatsop on the Oregon side of the river. Elk hunting was plentiful. They could easily make salt along the coast and settled down to survive a West Coast winter. By then, the expedition had used up almost all their supplies and given away most of their gifts. One ailment or another sickened many of the men. The weather was terrible—rainy, wet, icy, and bone-chillingly cold. The native Chinooks had adapted to the weather, but the Corps members were not used to it. Their clothing was always damp, to the point of being moldy. Firewood, too, was damp, causing smoky rather than blazing cooking fires. Everything was wet and rotting.

One year earlier, at Fort Mandan, the Corps received daily visitors. They got involved in the life of the Hidatsa and Mandan villages. Fort Clatsop, however, was a lonely and isolated place. The Corps did not receive many visitors or pay visits to the local tribesmen. Lewis and Clark felt little need to connect with the tribes, since the Northwest did not yet belong to the United States. Besides, they had nothing to negotiate and no goods to trade with the indigenous peoples. Fort Clatsop didn't interest the Chinooks either. White people and firearms did not impress them, especially since sailors with ammunition and trade goods had routinely landed in the area since the late 1780s. The Chinooks had seen more than one hundred fur-trading American ships on the Northwest Coast.[13]

On Christmas Day 1805, the weather was particularly miserable. The food had gone bad. But the Corps members exchanged a few gifts, such as moccasins, and baskets. Sacagawea gave Clark two dozen white weasel tails.[14] Lewis took advantage of the time and solitude. He collected plant and animal specimens that European Americans had never seen before. He wrote one-thousand-word essays to describe each one. Lewis also thought about how to give President Jefferson two pieces of bad news. Firstly, there was no northwest water passage, which meant there was no way to sail from the Atlantic Ocean to the Pacific. Secondly, the Rocky Mountains were monstrous compared to the Appalachians. Over the quiet winter months, Lewis contemplated how to deliver the truth about North America's landscape.

The Corps heard about a beached whale. Many of the Clatsop Indians went to collect oil and blubber from the animal. Lewis and Clark wanted to see the monster whale but did not go until January 7 due to bad weather. They planned for a three-day journey, there and back. Clark prepared two canoes and chose twelve men to go to the beach. He did not choose Sacagawea.

Sacagawea, however, was determined to go with them. She had never seen the ocean, much less a whale. She had come a long way. To be so close and not see the ocean would have been a huge disappointment.[15] She spoke up and asked to go with them. Clark allowed her to join the outing.

When they reached the beach, the whale was nothing but bones. The Clatsop had stripped the whale clean. The small team did not see a whale that day, but they saw its enormous skeleton. Clark purchased some of the blubber and oil from the tribe. That visit to the beach stood out as the most exciting event of the winter. And Sacagawea had realized her dream of seeing the ocean.

They returned to Fort Clatsop and resumed a dull daily routine. The Corps had achieved their goal. After reaching the Pacific Ocean, they just wanted to go back to the East Coast. For the third and last time, they waited for spring. At least three or four months passed before the weather turned warm enough for them to travel again.

Chapter 7

JOURNEY'S END

The Corps members were bored. The mission was over. The thought of trekking home the same way they came held no appeal. In 1792, explorer Robert Gray had discovered the Columbia River's entry into the Pacific Ocean. He reached the West Coast by sailing around Cape Horn and up the northwest coast.[1] Corps members hoped to return home the same way, by ship. But no large sailing ships landed on shore while they were there. They had to go home the way they came, by land.

Back Across the Bitterroots

In March, the Corps traveled up the Columbia River, fighting the strong current. They reunited with their friends the Nez Perce. As a favor, the tribe had cared for the Corps's horses over the winter. In April 1806, heavy snow still covered the mountains. The pass would not open for at least two more months. By June, the men grew impatient and restless. Snow or no snow, they would attempt to cross the Bitterroots. The snow was still piled high, ten feet (3 m) deep, but it was frozen solid. That made it hard enough to walk across. They just had one problem: They could not find the trail. They were forced to turn back.

The delay may have been lucky. Three young Nez Perce guides offered to lead them across. They were no more than twenty years old but skilled, honest, and respected. The traveling was intense and risky, like the first time they crossed the Lolo Pass. But the young guides had an excellent sense of distance and timing. Every day, they led the group to a safe campground with good grass for the horses to graze. They took them across the Bitterroot Mountains in six days, half the time it took before.[2] Without their expertise, the Corps may not have made it over the Rocky Mountains.

Near the Continental Divide, Lewis and Clark made a risky decision. They would split up into three small groups. Lewis took nine men to the Marias River. He sent three men on another route. Clark and the rest of the group, including Sacagawea, went to Yellowstone. They planned to meet at a point on the Missouri River. In that way, they could discover more terrain and create a more detailed map.

However, they would also be exposed to more risks. Traveling in small groups on the Great Plains was dangerous. Every tribe in the country feared the Blackfeet. Lewis and his group headed straight into their territory. One day, they woke to find half their horses had been stolen in the night. They found the tracks of a war party but failed to find their horses.

Clark's group suffered the same problem. Half their horses were stolen. Their trip went more smoothly, however, with Sacagawea as a guide. From present-day Bozeman, Montana, she showed them a route through the mountains that saved time. Clark's group reached Yellowstone in two days. The landscape was stunning, but natural hazards plagued them. A grizzly bear smelled their meat supply and chased them. A massive bison herd kept them awake at night with their grunts and bellows. Worst of all, mosquitoes swarmed the group. Their skin swelled and itched. Even baby Pomp's face was puffed and blistering.[3]

Lewis and his group suffered the same natural hazards. They also experienced the expedition's most unfortunate and violent encounter with a tribe. It ended badly. At dawn on July 27, 1806, along the Two Medicine River, noises awakened the Corps members. Eight Piegan Blackfeet Indians were stealing their rifles. The Corps members leapt up and fought to keep their weapons. Reubin Field stabbed an Indian to death. Lewis shot another and may have killed him. The Blackfeet ran away, but the Corps feared they would return with a larger war party. They raced, without stopping, to the Missouri River. [4]

Home Again

The three small Corps groups reunited along the Missouri River. Each had their stories to tell. A few weeks later, in August, the boats returned to the Hidatsa and Mandan villages. With her baby, Jean Baptiste, and her husband, Charbonneau, Sacagawea left the expedition. She had spent sixteen months with Lewis and Clark. Her part of the journey was over. Sacagawea was home.

Captain Clark had grown very fond of Jean Baptiste. Even before reaching St. Louis, he missed the baby he nicknamed Pomp. On August 20, 1806, Clark wrote a letter to Charbonneau. He made what might sound like an odd request. He offered to raise the child as his own son. He promised to educate him and treat him as a family member. He called him "my little dancing boy."[5] Sacagawea and Charbonneau considered Clark's offer, but they decided that baby Pomp was too young to leave his mother.

Lewis and Clark sailed into St. Louis on September 23, 1806. The people of St. Louis lined the river to welcome the heroes home. Many thought the captains' safe return surprising. More than two years had passed, after all. And no one had known their fate, whether they had lived or died.

Westward Expansion

Soon after the Lewis and Clark expedition, a period known as the Westward Expansion began. Steamboats provided new methods of water transportation, and roads formed. Pioneers drove covered wagons over rutted trails across the land. They formed caravans, one wagon following the other.

In 1848, the gold rush inspired a frenzy. People literally rushed west in search of gold. The first railroad was built in 1860. Two years later, Congress passed a new law. The Homestead Act encouraged pioneers to head west. The act granted settlers 160 acres (65 ha) of land for free if they lived on it for five years.[6] By 1890, the landscape in which Sacagawea once lived, and Lewis and Clark had explored, was changed.[7] The US government had ended the centuries-old Native way of life.

In the 1800s, hundreds of thousands of European settlers traveled west in wagon trains, seeking to claim land and build lives as farmers, ranchers, miners, or entrepreneurs.

"I received, my dear Sir, with unspeakable joy your letter of Sep. 23 announcing the return of yourself, Capt Clarke & your party in good health to St. Louis."[8]

— Thomas Jefferson to Lewis

After their return, the captains did a great deal of socializing. They attended dinners and dances, parties and balls, held in their honor. Lewis immediately wrote to Jefferson but did not divulge any stories from the trip. He wanted to tell the president about the journey in person. A few months later, he reached Washington DC. Lewis told the president the tales of his travels. It was a triumphant reunion.

Lewis told Jefferson all about his contact with the Native tribes. By the end of the journey, up to fifty-five tribes had come across the Corps of Discovery. Some tribes, such as the Crow (Absaroke), watched the expedition without ever being seen.[9] They may have feared the group of white strangers or believed they lacked firearms and other resources to take on members of the expedition, if necessary. While dozens of tribes encountered the Corps, only about sixteen had significant encounters with them.[10]

Mapping the Journey

Lewis and Jefferson studied the continent's geography. They spread maps out on the White House floor. They got down on their knees to study them in detail. Lewis finally broke the disappointing news to Jefferson that no fabled northwest water passage crossed the continent. Instead, the Corps had found an excellent overland route. He showed Jefferson where they had crossed the country by boat, on horseback, and on foot. He described the Rocky Mountains and the beaches of Oregon. He told him about the peaceful visits with many tribes. Lewis and Clark had explored the West. They made Jefferson's dream come true.

Lewis and Clark have been hailed as brave adventurers and heroes. They made an epic adventure through dangerous conditions. They explored and described, in detail, a wilderness that very few whites had ever seen. Native peoples allowed them into their homes, camps, and villages. And as captains, Lewis and Clark had led a disciplined team, kept morale high, and treated every Corps member with respect. The team worked well together for almost three years. For the most part, it was an enormously successful journey for the United States.

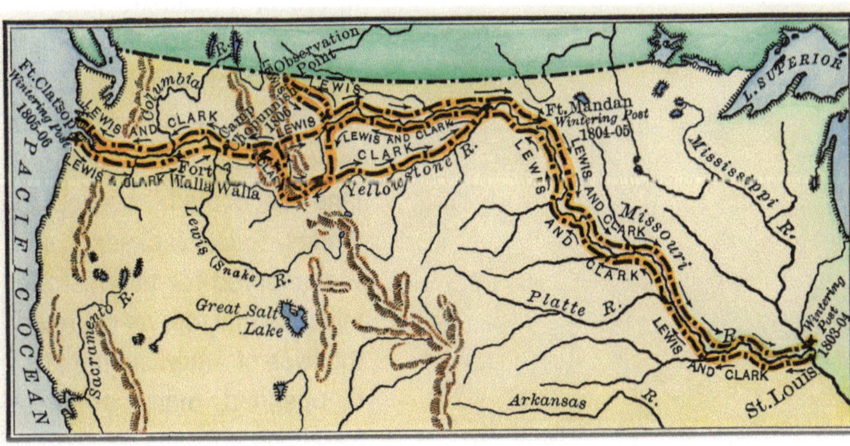

Lewis and Clark's remarkable journey took them 8,000 miles from the Missouri River to the Pacific Ocean and back.

The Indian Removal Act

East of the Mississippi River, the United States developed quickly. European Americans clashed with Native Americans. In 1830, President Andrew Jackson signed the Indian Removal Act. The law allowed the government to take tribal lands near white settlements. In exchange, the president gave Native peoples new tribal land west of the Mississippi. At first, a few tribes agreed to the exchange. During his presidency, Jackson signed seventy treaties. Fifty thousand American Indians moved West.

The Cherokee Nation refused to move. In 1838 and 1839, the United States government forced Cherokee people from their homes. Sixteen thousand Cherokee marched to new land. As many as four thousand died on the way. The tragic event is called the "Trail of Tears."[11]

In 1803, President Andrew Jackson signed the Indian Removal Act, which not only forced Native Americans to relocate but also granted land east of the Mississippi to whites. Today, Jackson is still remembered for this historic injustice that forever changed the lives of American Indians. It upended many of their traditions.

As payment for the mission, Lewis and Clark received large parcels of land and double the money they'd been promised. All of the men on the trip, except for York, earned a salary. Sacagawea received no pay as well. She had never been contracted to receive payment, but Clark knew that she deserved something. After all, her knowledge of two indigenous languages and of the landscape near the Shoshone had proven vital. Plus, her very presence had convinced the Nez Perce that the Corps had not come to attack them. In light of Sacagawea's contributions to the expedition, Clark wrote a letter to Charbonneau on August 20, 1806. He said, "your woman who accompanied you that long, dangerous and fatiguing rout [*sic*] deserved a greater reward."[12]

> ***"Your woman who accompanied you that long, dangerous and fatiguing rout [sic] deserved a greater reward."***[13]
>
> **— Clark**

Clark may have recognized that Sacagawea deserved pay for her services, but he does not appear to have given her a portion of his payment, or any other reward, to make up for the oversight. Sacagawea's husband did receive money and land for working as an interpreter on the trip, but she likely had no say in how he made use of his reward. In the end, two of the expedition's key members—York and Sacagawea—were shortchanged.

Chapter 8

THE MYTH BEGINS

The years after the great adventure proved difficult for Meriwether Lewis. Some of his biographers believe the captain had trouble adjusting. The expedition turned out to be an exciting adventure, but once it ended, his ordinary life may not have inspired him as much. Lewis also had many problems. He had long suffered from bouts of depression and also suffered from periods of alcoholism. This may not have been a coincidence, as a number of people with mental illness abuse alcohol and drugs to "self-medicate." Particularly in Lewis's day, people with depression may not have felt they had any option to treat their melancholy but to numb the pain. They did not live in a time when people visited therapists or could take a variety of prescription drugs to treat mood disorders.

Since whiskey was in short supply during the expedition, Lewis did not exhibit signs of alcoholism because he could not drink. The lack of liquor suited him well, since after returning to St. Louis and Washington DC, he began drinking heavily again.

Lewis had planned to write a book. He felt only then would the expedition be a true success. He considered his journals and papers from the trip among his most prized possessions. Although he desperately wanted the public to know about the expedition, he ran into obstacles as he tried to achieve this goal. He consulted with several publishers and even went into debt paying some of them. But three years passed, and nothing happened. Lewis did not have a published book about the expedition.

Lewis, Sacagawea, and Clark Die

Lewis also faced work-related stress after Jefferson appointed him governor of the Louisiana territory. The difficult job had little in common with exploration. One day his work duties required him to travel from St. Louis to Washington, DC, to settle some financial issues. Lewis stopped at an inn in Tennessee on October 11, 1809. As he climbed into bed, he complained of a fever.[1] That night, the innkeeper heard gunshots and rushed to his room. She found Lewis's body shot and stabbed. He'd died at the age of thirty-five.

While he may have been murdered, evidence also suggests that Lewis killed himself. Some believe a combination of factors led the explorer to die so young. They say he may have suffered from a painful illness like malaria and was mentally unstable, a condition that his alcoholism had no doubt worsened.

> *"It is with extreme pain that I have to inform you of the death of His Excellency Meriwether Lewis."*[2]
>
> **—James Neelly, Indian agent to the Chickasaw Nation, to Thomas Jefferson**

Not the First European Explorers

Sixty-five years before Lewis and Clark built Fort Mandan, a French Canadian fur trader visited the same Mandan and Hidatsa villages. Pierre Gaultier de Varennes et de la Vérendrye, born in 1685,[3] also searched for a northwest water passage to the Pacific Ocean. From Lake Winnipeg, he traveled south along the Missouri River. On December 3, 1738, he reached the villages. He was first to record his observations but not the first white person there. The Native peoples already had French and Spanish trade goods[4] in their possession. Before his death in 1749, La Vérendrye faced criticism for not finding the fabled Northwest Waterway. In 1800, over sixty years later, Sacagawea lived in those same villages. Three years later, Lewis and Clark spent the winter at Fort Mandan. They met Sacagawea, sealing their fate together.

Health problems and a fragile mental state could have left him vulnerable enough to commit suicide. Depression ran in his family, making him even more susceptible to suicide.

Reportedly, Sacagawea died after Lewis's untimely death. On December 20, 1812, a trading post clerk in present-day South Dakota wrote, "This evening the wife of Charbonneau, a Snake [Shoshone] squaw, died of a putrid fever. She was good and the best woman in the fort. Aged about 25 years. She left a fine infant girl."

Sacagawea fits the description and would have been that age. She had also recently given birth to a daughter, Lizette. Charbonneau, however, had five young Indian wives, making it difficult to know which wife had died. Her name would have

Prior to Lewis and Clark's expedition, French Canadian explorer Pierre Gaultier de Varennes traveled a similar route in search of the fabled Northwest water passage.

This monument to Lewis was built in 1848, almost forty years after his death on the Natchez Trace Parkway in Tennessee. Lewis died in mysterious circumstances.

been undeniable proof, but it was the convention of the time to refer to a woman with a simple noun such as "wife," or in the case of a Native American woman, "squaw." Because the clerk did not name the particular wife, his record does not prove that it was Sacagawea who succumbed to fever. If she did die that night in 1812, her body is buried in an unmarked grave.

William Clark would be the last of the three to die. In 1808, he married Julia Hancock. They had five children. He named his oldest son Meriwether Lewis Clark in honor of his friend and coexplorer. After Sacagawea reportedly died, Clark became the legal guardian of her son, Jean Baptiste, and served as the agent of Indian Affairs in the West. He also served as a brigadier general of the militia.

In 1813, he became governor of the Missouri Territory. He continued to encourage peace between the United States and Native peoples and made many friends among the various tribes. After seven years, however, he lost the position. People thought he sympathized too greatly with Native Americans. Even so, he assisted in the effort to remove tribes from their homelands, the effects of which still reverberate today. By forcing Native Americans out of the regions they'd called home for centuries, the US government effectively upended their way of life. Nomadic tribes could no longer freely roam, and others no longer had access to the animals they depended on for food, clothing, and housing. So while Clark may have been criticized for being too supportive of Native Americans, he ultimately backed US policy[5] detrimental to indigenous peoples.

After his wife died in 1820, Clark remarried and fathered two more children. He and Lewis reportedly each fathered children with Native American women as well. The father of many fell seriously ill on September 1, 1838. He died in St. Louis at the age of sixty-nine.[6]

Did Sacagawea Really Die in 1812?

Native American oral history disputes that Sacagawea died in 1812. Instead, Charbonneau's other wife, Otter Woman, may have perished from putrid fever, a form of typhus. Oral histories say that Charbonneau beat Sacagawea, so she left him. During the expedition, even members of the Corps of Discovery reportedly witnessed Charbonneau striking Sacagawea. If domestic violence did indeed cause the young Shoshone woman to flee, she completely vanished afterward, making her somewhat of a mystery.

In fact, for many years the public did not know her name. Expedition member William Gass published his journal in 1807 but never identified her, despite her important contributions to the journey. His omission meant that the story of Sacagawea could easily have disappeared from history.

But by the 1900s, Sacagawea's story began to take on mythic qualities. People regarded her as a heroine, even though many details of her life remain unknown. Because of public interest, authors and historians tried to find the missing information in her biography. In 1925, to clear up the mystery, the Bureau of Indian Affairs hired Dr. Charles Eastman, to investigate her story. Eastman, a Dakota Sioux, spoke with elderly people of many Native American tribes about the impressive Shoshone woman. Eastman's interviews with the Comanche in Wyoming, the Shoshone in Montana, and the Hidatsa in North Dakota proved especially helpful.

Through these conversations, Eastman learned that Sacagawea had assumed a new name—Porivo. She remarried, to a Comanche man. The union stood out because she chose and agreed to it; she loved her husband. They went on to have five children. After twenty-five years, her husband died, and she left the Comanche. She returned to her Shoshone people on the Wind River Reservation. There, she raised Jean Baptiste and her stepson, Bazile, the child of Otter Woman. During her life as Porivo, she told stories about helping the white men make a long journey. She owned a silver Jefferson peace medal. She verified information about the Lewis and Clark expedition, but she never made her part known publicly. Porivo died on April 9, 1884, and was buried at Fort Washakie in Wyoming.[7]

Dr. Eastman found many of these oral histories believable because they overlapped with one another. He could not dismiss the evidence. He concluded that Sacagawea had, indeed, gone on to live a long life. "We have to accept the tribal traditions," he wrote in his report. "We must accept it as the truth."

> *"We have to accept the tribal traditions. We must accept it as the truth."*
> **— Dr. Charles Eastman**

Lying is not customary in Shoshone culture, and Porivo had little reason to impersonate Sacagawea. She clearly did not do so for fame, because she made no public claim to her life as an explorer. To explain why she kept her story quiet, Eastman suggests that marrying Charbonneau and traveling with the Corps of Discovery wasn't her choice. "Fate seemed to have compelled her to live the life that she did,"[8] he wrote.

Sacagawea's grave sits in a remote and peaceful cemetery on the Wind River Indian Reservation in Wyoming. No road signs mark the way.

First Monument to Sacagawea

In 1905, Portland staged the first Lewis and Clark Centennial Exposition. The fair was less about Lewis and Clark and more about showing off new inventions. Over a million and a half visitors went to the fair. They saw moving picture shows, blimps, auto races, and electric lights.

The exposition did feature a bronze statue of Sacagawea and her son Jean Baptiste. It was the first monument to honor Sacagawea. Even though Sacagawea was not really a guide, artist Alice Cooper portrayed Sacagawea pointing the way west.

Today, the statue sits in Washington Park in Portland, Oregon. Since then, many statues and monuments have been installed to honor Sacagawea. Schools, community organizations, and geographical landmarks have also been named after her. Americans remember her for the heroic part she played in history.

The Lewis and Clark Centennial Exposition of 1905 drew attention to Portland, Oregon. Three million people visited the fair. Portland's population doubled over the next five years.

There are more than twenty Sacagawea statues across the United States. No other American woman has had so many statues built in her honor. This 1980 bronze statue of Sacagawea stands at the Buffalo Bill Center of the West in Cody, Wyoming.

In 1963, a monument honoring Sacagawea was installed on the Wind River Reservation. A bronze statue commemorates her first look at the Pacific Ocean. The Sacagawea statue holds a sand dollar, marking her beach trip. In real life, Sacagawea presented the creature as a gift to Shoshone Chief Washakie, and he wore it with honor in many historical pictures.[9]

If the oral history about Sacagawea is accurate, her gravesite sits between the graves of her son Jean Baptiste and her adopted son Bazil. Sacajawea Cemetery is in a remote location of the Wind River Reservation. No road signs guide the way.

Chapter

9

LEGACY

Lewis never published the book he planned to write. He died before he wrote a single page. In 1810, Nicholas Biddle edited the journals. He interviewed Clark to gather more information. Biddle's report got little attention, however. A period of rapid change marked the nineteenth century, and history books barely mentioned Lewis and Clark.

Why Were Lewis and Clark Ignored?

In 1889, Henry Adams wrote his nine-volume *History of the United States of America During the Administrations of Thomas Jefferson and James Madison, 1801–1817*. He only briefly mentioned Lewis and Clark in the series. In retrospect, the Corps of Discovery seemed like a small event, and the expedition journals ended up in storage at the American Philosophical Society in Philadelphia. By the end of the nineteenth century, people lost interest in Lewis and Clark, although a naturalist named Elliot Coues wrote an annotated version of Biddle's 1814 report. For eighty years, the public largely forgot about the expedition.

At last, in 1904 and 1905, historical writer Reuben G. Thwaites published a full edition of the Lewis and Clark journals in their original form—bad spelling, terrible punctuation, and all. This authentic edition of the Lewis and Clark journals sparked renewed interest in the expedition. Their century-old story began to be interpreted in new ways, with fresh perspectives. Historians began considering alternate viewpoints, viewpoints that included Sacagawea and her people. [1,2]

Sacagawea had no way of knowing that her life would be celebrated. In her lifetime, she was a typical Plains Indian woman. She did not use writing. She did not write down the details of her own story. The journals, letters, and diaries that the men of the expedition wrote are primary documents. Their notes about Sacagawea are considered accepted facts. Sometimes, Lewis and Clark expressed genuine concern and fondness for Sacagawea. At other times, their view of her was detached. Mostly, they disregarded her. They did not devote much journal space to an Indian woman and her child. Perhaps they did not consider how extraordinary her presence was on the expedition.

With so little primary source material to consult, Sacagawea's life story has been hard to fully know. For many historians, Lewis's and Clark's journal excerpts pose more questions than they answer about Sacagawea. What kind of personality did she have? What did she look like? Did she enjoy being part of the expedition? Historians have puzzled over the lack of information about her.

In 1902, Eva Emery Dye wrote and published *The Conquest: The True Story of Lewis and Clark.* Her book was historically accurate and based on fact. She conducted serious research. However, Dye wrote it like a novel, with a fast-paced and dramatic writing style. She romanticized the exciting story of the three explorers. She described Sacagawea as a beautiful Indian princess with shining eyes, sparkling necklaces, and long, flowing hair. Her book introduced Sacagawea to general readers for the first time. Dye's page-turning book became very popular.

Later, Dye worked to memorialize Sacagawea with statues. Her efforts helped to make Sacagawea an American icon.[3]

The story of Sacagawea grew to legendary proportions. In the early 1900s, Sacagawea came to represent many things. She symbolized peace and friendship. She also symbolized social change. She represented women's strength and leadership. The mythic figure of Sacagawea inspired the women's suffrage movement—the struggle of women to gain voting and other rights. Subsequent authors have used conjecture to guess at what might have happened during the expedition and what Sacagawea might have been like. Many fictionalized versions of her life story have been written.

The Native Perspective

Historians began to review the expedition from the point of view of Native Americans. One historian, James P. Ronda, wrote a book called *Lewis and Clark Among the Indians.* He suggested that some tribal behaviors confused Lewis and Clark. They described indigenous peoples from their own point of view and applied their European values to what they witnessed. Confronted by behaviors they did not understand, they tended to rely on stereotypes.

For example, when Lewis and Clark saw Native women hard at work, they concluded that women were mistreated. They accused Indian men of forcing women to do drudge work. But many tribes viewed women's roles as important and respected them. Lewis and Clark had difficulty considering that point of view. In white American culture, privileged women had few responsibilities.

Although Lewis and Clark worked to befriend tribal people, they also asked tribes to obey the United States government. In this way, the Lewis and Clark expedition initiated a period

Artists of the West

The Corps of Discovery did not hire an artist. Readers of Lewis's and Clark's journals can only imagine the adventures the captains describe. People long to imagine how the country looked when Sacagawea, Lewis, and Clark visited. Some artists have reimagined these scenes in paintings.

Born in St. Louis in 1864, Charles M. Russell was one such artist. Before the Montana transplant died in 1926, he created more than two thousand paintings of the old American West. One of his famous murals is called *Lewis and Clark Meeting the Flatheads at Ross's Hole.* Today, it hangs in Montana's capitol building in Helena.[4]

More recently, Charles Fritz painted more than one hundred images to illustrate the Lewis and Clark expedition. Born in 1955 and raised in Iowa, he now lives in Billings, Montana. He works outdoors, using the landscape as his artist's studio. His paintings have been praised for their historical accuracy.[5]

of sadness and loss for Native Americans. At the time, white Americans largely viewed Native peoples as obstacles to creating the United States.[6] Westward expansion led to the US we know today, but it also destroyed indigenous people's homelands. It ended a way of life that had existed for centuries.

Some historians have wondered if Lewis and Clark knew their mission would help to destroy Native ways of life. Robert J. Miller, from the Eastern Shawnee Tribe of Oklahoma, wrote a book called *Native America, Discovered and Conquered: Thomas Jefferson, Lewis and Clark, and Manifest Destiny*. A law professor at Lewis and Clark University in Portland, Oregon, until 2013, he proposed that Thomas Jefferson had set out to claim Native land

Artist Charles M. "Charlie" Russell (1864–1926) filled more than two thousand canvases with paintings of cowboys, Native Americans, and the old American West.

from the start. Miller believes Jefferson followed the Doctrine of Discovery. The doctrine stated that, by law, the first Europeans to arrive in a territory could claim to have discovered that land.

According to the doctrine, when Lewis and Clark planted a flag, they "discovered" the land, even though Native Americans had populated it for centuries. And when Lewis and Clark built forts, they owned the land by living on it. It did not matter that other people were already there. The Doctrine of Discovery supported the notion of European superiority. It also led to the rise in the 1840s of another principle—Manifest Destiny. This belief held that God had destined US expansion, which made it justifiable.[7]

Sacagawea's Heritage

Sacagawea State Park is by Pasco, Washington. It sits near where the Snake and Columbia Rivers meet. On that spot, Native peoples gathered, camped, fished, hunted, and traded for thousands of years. In that area, raiding warriors captured Sacagawea. On October 16, 1805, she returned to the same place with Lewis and Clark. Because of this history, the park hosts annual Sacagawea Heritage Days. The celebration includes reenactments of the expedition, and people can dress, camp, and eat in the way that Lewis, Clark, and Sacagawea did.

A similar festival takes place in Salmon, Idaho, near Sacagawea's birthplace. Every summer, the Sacagawea Interpretive, Cultural, and Educational Center hosts Agaidika Heritage Days. Festivalgoers can walk to Lemhi Pass, eat foods the Corps ate, and see a tribal dance exhibit. They can learn about blacksmithing, mapping, and many other activities from the early nineteenth century.

Although the land has changed, the public keeps the stories of Sacagawea, Lewis, and Clark alive. The federal government has also contributed to the expedition's legacy. In January 2001,

President Clinton held an important reception at the White House. He awarded William Clark the rank of US Army captain. He also made Sacajawea and York honorary sergeants. He bestowed honors on them that they did not receive during their lifetimes and likely could not have imagined.

Two women accepted the award on behalf of Sacagawea. They had personal connections with the Shoshone explorer. Rose Ann Abrahamson, is Agai-Dika, or Lemhi, Shoshone. She is a descendant of Chief Cameahwait, Sacagawea's brother. That makes Sacagawea her great-great-great aunt. Abrahamson is a teacher and a leading authority on Lemhi Shoshone cultural history.

In 2001, President Bill Clinton declared Sacagawea and York honorary sergeants of the Corps of Discovery. Rose Ann Abrahamson and Amy Mossett accompany Clinton.

An Excerpt from *The Conquest*

Eva Emery Dye's 1902 book, *The Conquest: The True Story of Lewis and Clark*, created a colorful version of the story. Toward the end of the journey, Dye described Sacagawea as she returned to her home in the Hidatsa village. The excerpt provides a sample of Dye's writing style. It illustrates the way she may have romanticized Sacagawea: "Sacajawea, modest princess of the Shoshones, heroine of the great expedition, stood with her babe in arms and smiled upon them from the shore. So had she stood in the Rocky Mountains pointing out the gates. So had she followed the great rivers, navigating the continent."[8]

In a radio interview, Abrahamson talked about the importance of Sacagawea's conversation with Clark on August 17, 1805. That day, Sacagawea told Clark through sign language that she was a Lemhi Shoshone. She expressed her identity to him. This was her nation.[9]

It has been important for Abrahamson to know her own identity as a Native American. "It's really wonderful to know who you are," she says, "and to know where you come from."[10] Perhaps that is one reason why Sacagawea's story is still so important today.

Amy Mossett, a nationally recognized Sacagawea expert, also appeared at the White House ceremony to accept the award. She belongs to the Mandan, Hidatsa, and Arikara Nation, or the Three Affiliated Tribes. She closely identifies with Sacagawea. And during the Lewis and Clark bicentennial commemoration, Mossett worked to make sure Native peoples were represented.

Eva Emery Dye's 1902 book *The Conquest: The True Story of Lewis and Clark* helped to preserve Sacagawea's story.

Sacagawea's granddaughter Mink Woman posed as a model for this statue. It is in the Capitol Building in Washington, DC.

> ***"In my mind, [Sacagawea] is not a myth. She is not a figment of someone's imagination. She was a young woman who lived in the same village as my ancestors."[11]***
>
> **—Amy Mossett**

When Mossett travels to speak about Sacagawea, she wears the clothing of an 1800s Hidatsa woman to portray Sacagawea during that time. Her ongoing mission is to depict Native American life accurately. She wants to preserve the way of life that Lewis and Clark witnessed. To collect research, she has visited with members of the Crow, Comanche, Lakota, Mandan, and Hidatsa Nations. Some are descended from the many tribesmen who met Lewis and Clark during the expedition. She has listened to several oral histories about Sacagawea, which she believes keep Sacagawea's story alive. As people remember Sacagawea, they continue to seek the truth about her life and contributions to the Corps of Discovery. Remembering her journey with Lewis and Clark helps people to understand both American history and the United States today.[12]

1770

William Clark is born in Virginia.

1774

Meriwether Lewis is born in Virginia.

1788

Sacagawea is born in Idaho into the Agaidiku tribe of the Shoshone.

1795

Lewis serves in the Chosen Rifle Company, commanded by Clark.

1801

Thomas Jefferson is voted third US president. Meriwether Lewis serves as his private secretary.

1803

Thomas Jefferson purchases the Louisiana Territory for fifteen million dollars from France, doubling the size of the United States.

Lewis and Clark spend the winter near St. Louis preparing for the trip.

1804

Lewis and Clark depart from Clarksville, Indiana Territory, beginning the Corps of Discovery.

1804

Sergeant Charles Floyd dies of a ruptured appendix. He is the only Corps member to die during the expedition.

Lewis and Clark have a dangerous conflict with the Teton Sioux. Chief Black Buffalo resolves the situation.

Lewis and Clark reach the Mandan and Hidatsa villages along the Missouri River. They decide to build Fort Mandan and spend the winter.

Sacagawea meets Lewis and Clark when her husband, Toussaint Charbonneau, a French-Canadian trapper and trader, brings her to Fort Mandan.

1805

Sacagawea gives birth to her son, Jean Baptiste Charbonneau, nicknamed "Pomp" by Clark.

The expedition leaves Fort Mandan.

Sacagawea is sick with fever and close to death; Clark and then Lewis treat her until she recovers.

Sacagawea, with Charbonneau and Clark, meets her Shoshone people, the first time she has seen them since her capture.

Lewis and Clark take a vote on where to locate Fort Clatsop. Every expedition member votes, including Sacagawea and York.

1806

Clark takes a small group to the ocean beach to see a whale that had washed up on shore. Sacagawea insists on being taken along. Clark agrees to her request.

The expedition returns to Fort Mandan. Sacagawea, her husband, and son stay.

Lewis and Clark return to St. Louis, Missouri.

1808

Clark marries Julia Hancock.

1809

Meriwether Lewis dies either of suicide or murder in a roadhouse by Natchez Trace. In 1846 a monument is placed at the site to honor him.

1812

Sacagawea reportedly dies of "putrid fever" at Fort Manuel, near Mobridge, South Dakota.

1838

William Clark dies in St. Louis, Missouri.

1884

Some believe Sacagawea actually died in 1884, having lived to a respectable old age.

1902

Eva Emery Dye publishes *The Conquest: The True Story of Lewis and Clark*, based partly on fact but embellished and romanticized with fiction. Interest in Sacagawea spikes.

1905–1906

The Lewis and Clark Centennial Exposition is held in Portland, Oregon.

2001

President Bill Clinton declares Sacagawea an honorary scout of the Corps of Discovery.

INTRODUCTION

1. James P. Ronda, *Lewis & Clark Among the Indians* (Lincoln, NE: University of Nebraska Press, 2002), chap. 8.

CHAPTER 1

Before the Corps

1. Patricia L. Zontine, "Lucy Meriwether Lewis Marks (1752–1837): Her Life and Her World," Monticello.org, April 2009, http://www.monticello.org/library/exhibits/lucymarks/lucymarks/lucy.html.
2. Jay H. Buckley, "William Clark: American Explorer," *Encyclopedia Britannica*, accessed December 27, 2017, http://www.britannica.com/biography/William-Clark.
3. Stephen E. Ambrose, *Undaunted Courage* (New York, NY: Simon and Schuster, 1996), p. 22.
4. Patricia L. Zontine, "Lucy Meriwether Lewis Marks (1752–1837): Her Life and Her World," Monticello.org, 2009, http://www.monticello.org/library/exhibits/lucymarks/lucymarks/lucy.html.
5. "Lemhi Shoshone Tribes," Lemhi-Shoshone.com, accessed December 27, 2017, http://www.lemhi-shoshone.com/.
6. Mae Parry, "The Northwestern Shoshone," Utah.gov, accessed December 27, 2017, http://historytogo.utah.gov/people/ethnic_cultures/the_history_of_utahs_american_indians/chapter2.html.
7. "An Introduction to the Wind River Indian Reservation of Wyoming," Jackson Hole Historical Society & Museum, accessed December 27, 2017, http://jacksonholehistory.org/an-introduction-to-the-wind-river-indian-reservation-of-wyoming/.
8. Ambrose, p. 40.

9. Frances Hunter, "The Court Martial of Meriwether Lewis," Frances Hunter's American Heroes Blog, January 2, 2012, http://franceshunter.wordpress.com/2012/01/02/the-court-martial-of-meriwether-lewis/.
10. Stephanie Krom, "The Whiskey Rebellion: An Interactive Mapping Project," Map the Rebellion, 2015, http://maptherebellion.com/.
11. Peter Kotowski, "Whiskey Rebellion," MountVernon.org, accessed December 27, 2017, http://www.mountvernon.org/digital-encyclopedia/article/whiskey-rebellion/.
12. Ambrose, pp. 134–136.
13. "William Clark to Meriwether Lewis, 18 July 1803," National Archives, June 29, 2017, http://founders.archives.gov/documents/Jefferson/01-41-02-0074-0002.
14. "Transcript: Jefferson's Secret Message to Congress," Library of Congress, accessed December 27, 2017, http://www.loc.gov/exhibits/lewisandclark/transcript56.html.

CHAPTER 2
Journey's Start

1. "Winter Among the Mandan," *National Geographic*, accessed December 27, 2017, http://www.nationalgeographic.com/lewisandclark/record_tribes_011_5_4.html.
2. "Missouri River," *Encyclopedia Britannica*, accessed December 27, 2017, http://www.britannica.com/place/Missouri-River.
3. "The Era of Westward Expansion," MissouriRiverWaterTrail.org, accessed December 27, 2017, http://missouririverwatertrail.org/river-history/era-western-expansion.
4. Joseph Mussulman, "Sacagawea Meets Lewis and Clark," Lewis-Clark.org, November 2005, http://www.lewis-clark.org/article/964.

5. Mae Parry, "The Northwestern Shoshone," Utah.gov, accessed December 27, 2017, http://historytogo.utah.gov/people/ethnic_cultures/the_history_of_utahs_american_indians/chapter2.html.
6. "An Introduction to the Wind River Indian Reservation of Wyoming," Jackson Hole Historical Society and Museum, accessed December 27, 2017, http://jacksonholehistory.org/an-introduction-to-the-wind-river-indian-reservation-of-wyoming/.
7. Tori Avey, "What Lewis and Clark Ate," PBS.org, May 31, 2013, http://www.pbs.org/food/the-history-kitchen/what-lewis-and-clark-ate/.
8. "Lewis and Clark Expedition: American Indians," National Park Service, accessed December 27, 2017, http://www.nps.gov/nr/travel/lewisandclark/indians.htm.
9. James John Holmberg, *Into the Wilderness: The Lewis and Clark Expedition* (Lexington, KY: University of Kentucky, 2003), pp. 14–15.
10. William E. Foley, *Wilderness Journey: The Life of William Clark*, (Columbia, MO: University of Missouri Press, 2004), p. 59.
11. James Holmberg, "Tribute to York," Kentucky Lewis and Clark Bicentennial Commission, October 14, 2003, http://www.lewisandclarkinkentucky.org/people/york_statue_remarks.shtml.
12. Stephen E. Ambrose, *Undaunted Courage* (New York, NY: Simon and Schuster, 1996), p. 138.
13. "Lewis: July 13, 1805," Journals of the Lewis and Clark Expedition, accessed December 27, 2017, http://lewisandclarkjournals.unl.edu/item/lc.jrn.1805-07-13.
14. Ambrose, pp. 188–189.

CHAPTER 3
Winter in the Mandan Village

1. James P. Ronda, *Lewis & Clark Among the Indians* (Lincoln, NE: University of Nebraska Press, 2002), pp. 28–41.
2. "MHA History: Epidemics," MHANation.com, accessed December 27, 2017, http://www.mhanation.com/main2/history/PDFs/Epidemics.pdf.
3. "Winter Among the Mandan, Mandan Indians, Part 5," Lewis and Clark Interactive Journey Log, *National Geographic*, accessed December 27, 2017, http://www.nationalgeographic.com/lewisandclark/record_tribes_010_5_3.html.
4. William E. Foley, *Wilderness Journey: The Life of William Clark* (Columbia, MO: University of Missouri Press, 2004), p. 93.
5. "Feb. 11, 1805," *Journals of the Lewis and Clark Expedition*, accessed December 27, 2017, http://lewisandclarkjournals.unl.edu/item/lc.jrn.1805-02-11.
6. Rebecca K. Jager, *Malinche, Pocahontas, and Sacagawea: Indian Women as Culture Intermediaries and National Symbols* (Norman, OK: University of Oklahoma Press, 2015), p. 83.
7. "The Mandan: History," MHANation.com, accessed December 27, 2017, http://www.mhanation.com/main2/history/PDFs/The%20Mandan.pdf.
8. William E. Foley, *Wilderness Journey: The Life of William Clark*, (Columbia, MO: University of Missouri Press, 2004), p. 93.

CHAPTER 4
Heading West

1. David J. Wishart, editor, "Lewis and Clark," *Encyclopedia of the Great Plains* (Lincoln, NE: University of Nebraska, 2011), http://plainshumanities.unl.edu/encyclopedia/doc/egp.ea.025.

2. "A Timeline of the Trip," PBS.org, accessed December 27, 2017, http://www.pbs.org/lewisandclark/archive/1805.html.
3. Barbara Fifer, "The Interpreter's Wife," Lewis-Clark.org, accessed December 27, 2017, http://www.lewis-clark.org/article/2667.
4. "January 5, 1806," Journals of the Lewis and Clark Expedition, accessed December 27, 2017, http://lewisandclarkjournals.unl.edu/item/lc.jrn.1806-01-05.
5. Journals of the Lewis and Clark Expedition, accessed December 27, 2017, http://lewisandclarkjournals.unl.edu/item/lc.about.faq.
6. Alan Reed, "Mossett Brings Respect to Sacagawea," Nathpo.org, Nov. 30, 2002, http://www.nathpo.org/News/Lewis_Clark/News_Lewis12.htm.
7. Journals of the Lewis and Clark Expedition, accessed December 27, 2017, http://lewisandclarkjournals.unl.edu/item/lc.jrn.1805-05-20.
8. "The Lewis and Clark Expedition Meets Medical and Health Challenges as They Go West," Medicine and Health on the Lewis and Clark Expedition, accessed December 27, 2017, http://exhibits.hsl.virginia.edu/lewisclark/journey/.
9. Stephen E. Ambrose, *Undaunted Courage* (New York, NY: Simon and Schuster, 1996), p. 89.
10. Marissa Fessenden, "How to Reconstruct Lewis and Clark's Journey: Follow the Mercury-laden Latrine Pits," Smithsonian.com, Sept. 8, 2015, http://www.smithsonianmag.com/smart-news/how-reconstruct-lewis-and-clark-journey-follow-mercury-laden-latrine-pits-180956518/.

CHAPTER 5

Meeting the Shoshone

1. "July 28, 1805," Journals of the Lewis and Clark Expedition, accessed December 27, 2017, http://lewisandclarkjournals.unl.edu/item/lc.jrn.1805-07-28.
2. Joseph Mussulman, "Lemhi Pass: A Gap in a Dividing Ridge," Lewis-Clark.org, September, 2009, http://www.lewis-clark.org/article/1779.
3. "Lemhi Pass," VisitMT.com, 2017, http://www.visitmt.com/listings/general/national-historic-site/lemhi-pass.html.
4. Stephen E. Ambrose, *Undaunted Courage* (New York, NY: Simon and Schuster, 1996), pp. 268–269.
5. Lara Marks, "Lewis and Clark Speak: Excerpts from Their Journal Entries About Sacajawea," Discrete Math with Proof, December 16, 1998, http://www.mathcs.bethel.edu/~gossett/DiscreteMathWithProof/sacajawea/quotes.html.
6. "The Conflict at Bear River: Primary Sources," Utah.gov, accessed December 27, 2017, http://ilovehistory.utah.gov/topics/primary_docs/bear_river/index.html.
7. "Lemhi Shoshone Tribes," Lemhi-Shoshone.com, accessed December 27, 2017, http://www.lemhi-shoshone.com/.
8. "Federal and State Recognized Tribes," NCSL.org, October 2016, http://www.ncsl.org/research/state-tribal-institute/list-of-federal-and-state-recognized-tribes.aspx.
9. Ambrose, p. 206.
10. James P. Ronda, *Lewis & Clark Among the Indians* (Lincoln, NE: University of Nebraska Press, 2002), pp. 147–148.

CHAPTER 6
Over the Rockies

1. Meghan Saar, "Fighting to Cross an Unknown America," *True West Magazine*, August 18, 2015, http://truewestmagazine.com/fighting-to-cross-an-unknown-america/.
2. "Deadly Crossing: The Bitterroots," *National Geographic*, accessed December 27, 2017, http://www.nationalgeographic.com/lewisandclark/journey_leg_12_11.html.
3. Joseph Mussulman, "Meeting the Salish at Ross Hole," Lewis-Clark.org, June 1998, http://www.lewis-clark.org/article/1157.
4. James P. Ronda, *Lewis & Clark Among the Indians* (Lincoln, NE: University of Nebraska Press, 1984), chap. 6, http://lewisandclarkjournals.unl.edu/item/lc.sup.ronda.01.06.
5. Ronda, p. 157.
6. "September 16, 1805," Journals of the Lewis and Clark Expedition, accessed December 27, 2017, http://lewisandclarkjournals.unl.edu/item/lc.jrn.1805-09-16.
7. Ronda, pp. 158–159.
8. Aaron Thelson, "Crossing Lolo Pass," *Northwest Travel and Life*, May 9, 2017, http://nwtravelmag.com/crossing-lolo-pass/.
9. Margaret Talbot, "Searching for Sacagawea," *National Geographic*, February 2003, http://ngm.nationalgeographic.com/ngm/0302/feature4/fulltext.html.
10. Stephen E. Ambrose, *Undaunted Courage* (New York, NY: Simon and Schuster, 1996), pp. 294–297.
11. Ambrose, p. 295.
12. "Lewis and Clark Timeline," LewisandClarkTrail.com, 1998, http://lewisandclarktrail.com/section2/ndcities/timeline1805.htm.

13. Ronda, introduction.
14. "Lewis and Clark Timeline 1805," National Park Service, April 10, 2015, http://www.nps.gov/jeff/learn/historyculture/lewis-and-clark-timeline-1805.htm.
15. "Lost America," Frances Hunter's American Heroes Blog, November 26, 2012, http://franceshunter.wordpress.com/.

CHAPTER 7
Journey's End

1. "Robert Gray: American Explorer," *Encyclopedia Britannica*, accessed December 27, 2017, http://www.britannica.com/biography/Robert-Gray-American-explorer.
2. Stephen E. Ambrose, *Undaunted Courage* (New York, NY: Simon and Schuster, 1996), pp. 362–364.
3. William E. Foley, *Wilderness Journey: The Life of William Clark* (Columbia, MO: University of Missouri Press, 2004), pp. 144–145.
4. Meghan Saar, "Fighting to Cross an Unknown America," *True West Magazine*, August 18, 2015, http://truewestmagazine.com/fighting-to-cross-an-unknown-america/.
5. Ambrose, pp. 380–384.
6. "Homestead Act," The Library of Congress, accessed December 27, 2017, http://www.loc.gov/rr/program/bib/ourdocs/Homestead.html.
7. Rebecca K. Jager, *Malinche, Pocahontas, and Sacagawea: Indian Women as Culture Intermediaries and National Symbols* (Norman, OK: University of Oklahoma Press, 2015), p. 250.
8. Mikki Meek, "The Story of Jean Baptiste," *National Geographic*, accessed December 27, 2017, http://ngm.nationalgeographic.com/ngm/0302/feature4/online_extra.html.

9. "The Native Americans," PBS.org, accessed December 27, 2017, http://www.pbs.org/lewisandclark/native/.
10. Ibid.
11. "Milestones 1830–1860," US Department of State, accessed December 27, 2017, http://history.state.gov/milestones/1830-1860/indian-treaties.
12. Stephenie Ambrose Tubbs, "Sacagawea," Oregon Encyclopedia.org, June 15, 2017.
13. Ibid.

CHAPTER 8

The Myth Begins

1. "Meriwether Lewis," Encyclopedia.com, accessed December 27, 2017, 2004, http://www.encyclopedia.com/people/history/us-history-biographies/meriwether-lewis.
2. "Lewis and Clark: The Journey Ends," *Smithsonian Magazine*, December, 2005, http://www.smithsonianmag.com/history/lewis-and-clark-the-journey-ends-110100664/.
3. "Pierre Gaultier de Varennes et de La Vérendrye 1732-1739," Virtual Museum of New France, Canadian Museum of History, accessed December 27, 2017, http://www.historymuseum.ca/virtual-museum-of-new-france/the-explorers/pierre-gaultier-de-varennes-et-de-la-verendrye 1732 1739/.
4. James P. Ronda, *Lewis & Clark Among the Indians* (Lincoln, NE: University of Nebraska Press, 2002), p. 73.
5. Jay H. Buckley, "William Clark: American Explorer," *Encyclopedia Britannica*, accessed December 27, 2017, http://www.britannica.com/biography/William-Clark.
6. Calvin and Rosanna Hamilton, "William Clark Biography," *Science Views*, accessed December 27, 2017, http://scienceviews.com/historical/williamclark.html.

7. Brian Altonen, "Eastman's Letter – Sacajawea's Grave," accessed December 27, 2017, http://brianaltonenmph.com/6-medical-anthropology/charles-eastman/.
8. Ibid.
9. "Sacagawea's Gravesite is Off-the-Beaten-Path," YellowstonePark.com, May 9, 2014, http://www.yellowstonepark.com/things-to-do/sacajawea-secret-gravesite.

CHAPTER 9
Legacy

1. Natasha Geiling, "Lewis and Clark Only Became Popular 50 Years Ago," *Smithsonian Magazine*, June 5, 2014, http://www.smithsonianmag.com/history/what-did-lewis-and-clark-expect-find-180951467/.
2. Anthony Brandt, "Sex, Dog Meat, and the Lash: Odd Facts about Lewis and Clark," *National Geographic*, December 8, 2003, http://news.nationalgeographic.com/news/2003/12/1204_031204_lewisclark.html.
3. Sheri Bartlett Browne, "Eva Emery Dye: Romance with the West," Oregon State University Press, accessed December 27, 2017, http://osupress.oregonstate.edu/book/eva-emery-dye.
4. "Charlie Russell's Paintings of the Corps of Discovery," Frances Hunter's American Heroes Blog, December 9, 2009, http://franceshunter.wordpress.com/2009/12/09/charlie-russells-lewis-clark-art/.
5. "Charles J. Fritz," Charles Fritz.com, accessed December 27, 2017, http://charlesfritz.com/about.php.
6. Rebecca K. Jager, *Malinche, Pocahontas, and Sacagawea: Indian Women as Culture Intermediaries and National Symbols* (Norman, OK: University of Oklahoma Press, 2015), p. 248.

7. Robert J. Miller, *Native America, Discovered and Conquered: Thomas Jefferson, Lewis and Clark, and Manifest Destiny* (Lincoln, NE: Bison Books, University of Nebraska Press, 2008), p. 174.
8. Eva Emery Dye, *The Conquest: The True Story of Lewis and Clark*, Gutenberg.org, accessed December 27, 2017.
9. "Episode 102: Sacagawea's Story, An American Mythology," *Unfinished Journey: The Lewis and Clark Expedition*, OPB.org, http://www.opb.org/programs/lewisandclark/transcripts/LC103.pdf.
10. "Rose Ann Abrahamson (Lemhi Shoshone/Bannock)," Museum of California, March 2011, http://www.youtube.com/watch?v=y5a9sHbVRJc.
11. Alan Reed, "Mossett Brings Respect to Sacagawea," Nathpo.org, Nov. 30, 2002, http://www.nathpo.org/News/Lewis_Clark/News_Lewis12.htm.
12. "American Indian Voices," C-Span.org, January 17, 2003, http://www.c-span.org/video/?174857-1/american-indian-voices.

biography A written history of someone's life authored by someone else.

confluence Joining of two or more streams flowing together at one meeting point.

conjecture To form an opinion based on incomplete information; to guess.

continental divide A natural border, also called a drainage divide, that separates waters that flow east from waters that flow west.

diplomacy The skill of a representative of one culture or state to negotiate with another foreign culture or state.

ethnography A branch of anthropology; the systematic study of peoples and culture.

keelboat Large flat-bottomed boat used to carry an expedition's supply of goods.

laudanum Painkiller containing opium.

miscreant A criminal, a person who is intentionally hurtful.

nomadic The quality of moving from place to place rather than living in one fixed location.

pirogues Canoes carved of tree trunks.

portage To carry a boat between two waterways.

primogeniture A law allowing a family's wealth to pass down only to the firstborn son.

sovereignty The authority of a state to govern itself or another state.

tributary One stream or river that feeds into a larger stream or river.

uncharted An area of land that is not mapped and has never been surveyed.

vermilion Bright red powder made from cinnabar, prized by Native peoples.

BOOKS

Edwards, Judith. *The Journey of Lewis and Clark in United States History*. New York: NY, Enslow Publishing, 2014.

Jones, Landon Y, editor. *The Essential Lewis and Clark.* New York, NY: The Ecco Press, 2000.

Sanford, William R., and Carl R. Green. *Sacagawea: Courageous American Indian Guide*. New York: NY, Enslow Publishing, 2012.

Thomasma, Kenneth. *Naya Nuki: Shoshoni Girl Who Ran.* Jackson, WY: Grandview Publishing Company, 2008.

WEBSITES

Discovering Lewis & Clark
http://www.lewis-clark.org/
A profile of the two explorers.

Women of the Fur Trade
http://womenofthefurtrade.com/home.php
A look at Sacagawea's life with a white fur trader.

FILMS

The West (2001)